GLOBETROTTER™

Travel Guide

KV-510-707

FLORENCE
AND TUSCANY

CAROLINE KOUBÉ

NEW
HOLLAND

NEW
HOLLAND

★★★ Highly recommended
★★ Recommended
★ See if you can

First edition published in 2001
by New Holland Publishers (UK) Ltd
London • Cape Town • Sydney • Auckland
10 9 8 7 6 5 4 3 2 1

Garfield House, 86 Edgware Road
London W2 2EA
United Kingdom

80 McKenzie Street
Cape Town 8001
South Africa

14 Aquatic Drive
Frenchs Forest NSW 2086
Australia

218 Lake Road, Northcote
Auckland
New Zealand

Distributed in the USA by
The Globe Pequot Press
Connecticut

ISBN 1 85974 646 2

Manager Globetrotter Maps: John Loubser
Managing Editor: Thea Grobbelaar
Editor: Thea Grobbelaar
Design and DTP: Lellyn Creamer
Cartographer: Nicole Engeler
Compiler/Verifier: Elaine Fick
Consultants: Katerina and Eric Roberts
Picture Researcher: Colleen Abrahams
Proofreader: Claudia Dos Santos
Reproduction by Hirt & Carter (Pty) Ltd, Cape Town
Printed and bound in Hong Kong by Sing Cheong
Printing Co. Ltd.

Photographic Credits:
Mark Azavedo: pages 28, 29, 74, 116, 118;
Paul Bernhardt: cover, title page, pages 4, 20, 46;
The Hutchison Library/John Hatt: pages 36, 37, 38;
The Hutchison Library/Tony Souter: pages 96, 97;
Image-Link: pages 6, 7, 8, 9 (top), 12, 13, 15, 18,
19, 21, 23, 24, 25, 27, 33, 35, 40, 44, 45, 47, 48, 50,
51, 52, 53, 54, 55, 61, 64, 65, 66, 68, 75, 77, 79, 80,
81, 82, 84, 85, 90, 91, 92, 99, 100, 101, 106, 107, 108,
109, 112, 114, 115;
Life File/Su Davies: page 98;
Life File/Emma Lee: page 9 (bottom);
Life File/Nigel Shuttleworth: page 83;
Life File/Giles Stokoe: page 26;
Life File/Andrew Ward: pages 30, 43;
Richard Sale: pages 10, 11, 14, 16, 22, 34, 39, 42,
58, 62, 63, 70, 72, 78, 88, 95, 104, 110, 117, 119;
Gregory Wrona: page 49.

Although every effort has been made to ensure accuracy
of facts, telephone and fax numbers in this book, the
publishers will not be held responsible for changes that
occur at the time of going to press.

Cover: *The cupola of the Duomo, Florence.*
Title Page: *Ammannati's Fountain of Neptune,*
Piazza della Signoria, Florence.

CONTENTS

1
Introducing
Florence and Tuscany

If we were to create a picture of perfection, starting with rolling hills and fertile valleys, a gentle and sometimes ethereal light, warm climate, bounteous cuisine, a cellar of fine wines, and we were then to fill it with some of man's most elegant buildings, decorated with astonishingly beautiful sculptures and paintings, and under their roofs housing some great literary works, we would have recreated Tuscany. For in this region Nature provided, and Man complemented.

It was in Tuscany's unique environment that modern Italy took form, that the Renaissance flowered thanks to the sponsorship of a few wealthy families, and that modern art and architecture put down their roots.

The extraordinary surge of creation, unparalleled not only elsewhere in Italy, but throughout the whole of Europe, has indelibly marked Tuscany, and in particular Florence.

It is this historic legacy which brings us to the region and in doing so permits us to discover a number of other magnificent towns which are likewise preserved for posterity. It enables us to witness historic pageants; to travel through the undulating landscape of wheat, vines and groves of olives, defined at times by dark cypress trees; to stop at Chianti's vineyards and taste the magnificent wine, or to linger over a Tuscan lunch in the shadow of Etruscan remains. And it introduces us to a history that itself gave birth to the Italian culture, long before the Renaissance spread through Tuscany and perfected this valuable legacy.

Top Attractions

*** The Uffizi Gallery: in Florence, it has a magnificent collection of paintings.
*** Siena: visit its Duomo, and also see the *Palio*.
*** Museo Nazionale del Bargello: in Florence, Italy's best collection of sculpture.
*** San Gimignano: with its 13 medieval towers.
** Pisa: see the famous Leaning tower and Cathedral.
** View of Florence: from the Campanile or Duomo.
** Isola d'Elba: in the steps of Napoleon, visit this island.
* Chianti: take a trip through the wine-growing region.

Opposite: *Like a guiding beacon, the Duomo's cupola is the heart of Florence.*

TUSCANY FACTS AND FIGURES

Area: approximately 23,000km² (8878 sq miles)
Population: approximately 3,473,000
Largest towns:
Florence (376,760 inhabitants), Prato (171,135 inhabitants), Pisa (92,494 inhabitants), Pistoia (85,906 inhabitants), Lucca (85,558 inhabitants), Grosseto (72,539 inhabitants) and Siena (54,436 inhabitants)
Airports: Pisa (international) and Florence (smaller)
Highest mountain: Mount Amiata, 1738m (5794ft)
Longest river: Arno, 241km (150 miles)
Coastline: over 300km (185 miles) long
Offshore islands: seven, of which Elba is largest

THE LAND

Many a poetic word has been dedicated to the lyrical countryside of Tuscany. The area is one of natural beauty, stretching from the **Apennine Mountains** – the backbone of Italy – in the east, down to the **Tyrrhenian Sea** in the west, and from the **Alpi Apuani** (the **Apuan Alps**) in the north to the political boundary with the province of Lazio, in the south. It is one of Italy's larger regions, extending over some 23,000km² (nearly 9000 sq miles), and one of its most visited. Roughly at its centre lies Siena, some 140km (87 miles) as the crow flies from the northern and southern extremes of Tuscany.

Coast

The Tuscan region has over 300km (185 miles) of mainland coastline. It also boasts seven islands, the **Archipelago Toscano**, in part protected by the statutes of a national park. Three of these islands are open to visitors. The largest is **Isola d'Elba** (223km² or 86 sq miles), followed by **Isola del Giglio** (21.2km² or 8 sq miles) and **Isola di Capraia** (19.5km² or 7 sq miles). The **Isola di Montecristo** is not open to visitors – it is a nature reserve – but it was this island which gave its name to Alexandre Dumas's famous fictional Count.

Beaches

The best natural beaches are found on the islands and in the Maremma (in the Monti dell'Uccellina, Uccellina Hills area of the **Parco Naturale della Maremma**). However,

Below: One of the country's prime sea resorts, Viareggio not only boasts fine sandy beaches, but interesting Liberty-style architecture.

the Tuscans prefer their beaches organized and the nearest sandy shore to the inland cities has become a series of beach clubs, each with restaurant, changing facilities, lines of neat parasols and *straie* (beach beds) so that sunworshippers may

socialize in comfort. The resorts of **Viareggio** and **Forte dei Marmi** in the north and **Punta Ala** in the south are the most prestigious while the **Marina di Pietrasanta**, **Lido di Camaiore** and, much further south, **Talamone**, are all favourites.

Mountains

The highest peak in Tuscany is the volcanic **Mount Amiata** at 1738m (5794ft), in the southeast part of the region, while the highest peak on Isola d'Elba is **Mount Capanne** at 1018m (3393ft). The relatively small, 635m (2100ft) **Mount Argentario** rises almost directly from the sea (it was formerly an island) but is attached by wisps of sandspits to the Maremma. Some hilly areas of note include the **Apuan Alps**, north of Lucca, known for their fine quality marble; the mineral-rich **Colline Metallifere** (**Metalliferous Hills**) between Siena and Massa Marittima; the limestone **Monti dell'Uccellina** (**Uccellina Hills**) which form a part of the Maremma; the odd *balze*, eroded crags near Volterra, the bare peaks, or *crete*, just south of Siena, and the **Chianti Hills**, a clay–rich area ideal for viticulture.

Tuscany also has a number of beautiful valleys enveloped in the folds of its hills, but no lakes of any size.

The valleys between the Chianti Hills are probably the best known, thanks to the wine that is produced there, but there is also the **Val d'Elsa**, along the River Elsa, the **Val di Chiana**, or Chiana Valley, which extends due south from near Arezzo to the Umbrian border, and the **Mugello**, the valley of the River Sieve, located to the north of Florence.

Above: *The variety of scenery in central Tuscany, such as this in the Val d'Orcia, has attracted a number of poets, painters and writers, and now beckons many northern Europeans to settle in its ancient villages and lovingly restored farmhouses.*

FLORENCE	J	F	M	A	M	J	J	A	S	O	N	D
MAX TEMP. °C	14	16	21	25	28	31	36	32	31	26	21	14
MIN TEMP. °C	6	8	9	13	16	17	20	18	17	14	9	6
MAX TEMP. °F	57	61	70	77	82	88	97	90	88	79	70	57
MIN TEMP. °F	43	46	48	55	61	63	68	64	63	57	48	43
HOURS OF SUN DAILY	4	5	6	6	7	9	9	9	7	6	4	3
RAINFALL mm	62	60	68	69	72	56	23	48	84	100	104	77
RAINFALL in	2.4	2.3	2.6	2.7	2.8	2.1	0.9	1.8	3.3	3.9	4.0	3.0
DAYS OF RAINFALL	8	8	8	8	7	4	3	3	5	9	10	11

Above: Early morning light touches the earthy colours of Florence's Ponte Vecchio.

Rivers

The most important river in Tuscany is the **River Arno**, 241km (150 miles) long. It rises on Mount Falterona, 1654m (5514ft) high, and is supplemented by the waters of north-flowing **River Elsa** and the south-flowing **River Sieve**. The Arno has cut a swathe through the western flanks of the Apennine Mountains and turns, just to the east of Florence, to flow westwards out to sea, some 12km (7.5 miles) beyond Pisa. Indeed, in Medieval days, Pisa was a marine power but silting over the centuries has forced it to turn to other trading activities. The Arno made headlines in 1966 when, during **torrential storms**, the river rose some 3m (10ft) above its normal level causing catastrophic damage to Florence and its art works. Subsequently, the river has been monitored rather like the heart of a premature baby and every possible rise in height is heralded by computer warnings.

Climate

Tuscany largely enjoys a Mediterranean climate though with altitude, in the hills and Apennine Mountains, this is tempered and the climate is somewhat cooler with more precipitation. Indeed, during the **warm summer** months the most pleasant place to be is at a slight altitude in the hills. **Winters** are generally cool at 8–14°C (47–57°F), with slightly more winter rainfall during November and December. **Spring** is unpredictable: it can be rainy, but will also be sunny. Summer, from June to early September, is warm at 18–25°C (68–78°F), peaking at around 30°C (86°F) in the hot summer afternoons, and rainfall is rarely more than a short and sharp thunder shower. **Autumn** is a very pleasant time – the days are shorter, temperatures are lower, but the weather is generally dry.

Flora and Fauna

From stark snow-capped peaks in winter to almost subtropical warmth on the summer coast, Tuscany has a wide range of flora and fauna. There are two national parks and three regional parks, all designed to protect the environment.

Tuscany is a zone of fine, natural woods, some of Italy's best preserved. Where man has not neatly arranged nature with his vineyards, olive groves, corn and wheat, **evergreens** such as cypress (originally introduced by man) and cork oak thrive. The coastal areas have beautiful **pine forests** – both umbrella and maritime pines – while the hills of Tuscany are known for their proliferation of **wild flowers**: scarlet poppies, mauve scabious, blue cornflowers, yellow broom, pink peas and white cistus. In the less humid areas of the *gariga*, fragrant herbs, rosemary, myrtle and prickly pears thrive. Up in the mountains, beech, oak, chestnut, ash and poplar trees dominate the **forests**.

Hunting has decimated much of the larger fauna in Tuscany but the smaller mammals and birds are sustained by the large tracts of wild and semi-wild countryside. Rabbits, weasels, foxes, martens, hedgehogs, porcupines and wild boar are numerous while there are some (originally imported) deer in the less populated Maremma region. This area is known for its sheep and cattle rearing, and there are herds of horses. **Golden eagles**, **kites**, **buzzards** and nocturnal **owls** share the skies with plenty of **migratory birds** such as the swift, nightingale and cuckoo, while waterfowl like egrets, cranes, geese and ducks favour the estuaries and shore.

Above: *Brilliant sunflowers splash the southern Tuscan landscape in the summer time.*
Below: *The profusion of wild flowers makes Tuscany a popular place for springtime ramblers.*

HISTORY IN BRIEF

The history of Tuscany is one of great culture – first displayed under the Etruscans and reaching its zenith during the Renaissance – and that of municipal rivalry between its famous towns. **Etruria** was the earliest Italian civilization, later absorbed into the **Roman Empire**. Numerous Roman **colonies** were founded, and these blossomed into powerful **city-states** during the Middle Ages. Pre-eminent of these was **Florence**, cultural and commercial bastion and birthplace of the **Renaissance**. Tuscany then languished along with the rest of Italy until its rediscovery by 18th-century tourists. Since then, apart from a brief stint when Florence became the capital of the new kingdom of Italy, Tuscany has been preserving history rather than making it.

First Settlers

The plain of the Arno is thought to have been inhabited since Neolithic times (about 10,000BC) but the first real archaeological evidence of settlement comprises pottery shards from Pisa dating from approximately 5500BC. Farmers and herdsmen appeared in the Tuscan hills and valleys around 1600BC and the use of iron occurred some time around 1100BC.

Below: *Fiesole has one of Tuscany's best preserved Roman theatres.*

Etruscans

Scholars have always been divided over whether the Etruscans were indigenous to Italy, or came from Asia Minor after the Trojan War. Whatever their origins, the Etruscans flourished around 800BC in the **coastal regions** of modern Tuscany and Lazio, establishing agriculture, far-reaching trading links and a thriving economy based on **mineral**

wealth. Metals were worked into fine objects and exchanged for luxury goods.

The Etruscans dominated the whole of modern Tuscany and a large area of central Italy, including Rome, up to the sixth century BC, and Tuscany is littered with the remains of Etruscan villages, statuary and

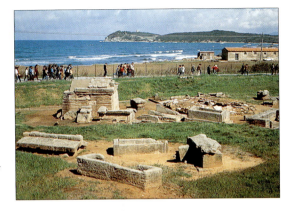

tombs. There was no centralized empire, however, though the 12 main city-states (thought to include Fiesole, Chiusi, Cortona, Arezzo and Volterra) were loosely grouped together, mainly for religious purposes, in a confederation known as the **Dodecapolis**. Rome in its infancy was ruled by the Tarquin dynasty of Etruscan kings until **Tarquinius Superbus** was driven out in 509BC.

Above: *Populonia was once a major Etruscan port. Its necropolis is of major archaeological interest.*

HISTORICAL CALENDAR

ca. 5500BC Evidence of settlement at Pisa.
ca. 800BC Etruscan civilization flourishes.
5th century BC Rome begins conquest of central Italy.
59BC Florence founded by Julius Caesar for army veterans.
AD476 The Roman Western Empire ends.
568 The Lombards set up camp in Lucca.
800 Charlemagne crowned Holy Roman Emperor.
1115 Countess Matilda of Tuscany dies.
1296 Building is begun on Florence cathedral.
1347 Black Death sweeps through Europe.

1378 *Ciompi* rebellion.
1406 Florence conquers Pisa.
1434 Cosimo de Medici gains power in Florence.
1478 Pazzi conspiracy.
1494 The Medici expelled from Florence.
1497 Bonfire of the Vanities in Florence.
1512 Return of the Medici.
1557 Siena falls to Florence.
1570 Cosimo I becomes Grand Duke of Tuscany.
1737 Control of Tuscany passes to Austrian Hapsburgs.
1798 Napoleon invades Tuscany and creates the kingdom of Etruria.
1814–15 Napoleon is exiled on the island of Elba.

1847 Lucca last city-state to become part of Tuscany.
1848 Revolution sweeps across Europe.
1861 Unification of Italy under the House of Piedmont; Florence becomes capital city.
1871 Rome becomes the capital of Italy.
1915 Italy joins the Allies in World War I.
1922 Fascists march on Rome and Mussolini takes over.
1940 Italy enters World War II on the side of Germany.
1944 Allies reach Florence.
1946 End of monarchy. Italy becomes a republic.
1966 Great Flood in Florence.
1993 Uffizi bomb in Florence.

Above: *The famous Leaning Tower will soon lean less, thanks to conservation efforts.*
Opposite: *A beautiful* Madonna and Child *by master sculptor Donatello.*

RECOGNIZE THE BRIDGE?

You may not, at first sight. But look again at a reproduction of the *Mona Lisa* and there, behind the mysterious sitter, is Buriano Bridge, one of the bridges that span the Arno and which was first built in 1179. This famous bridge is located along the route between Florence and Arezzo, on the so-called 'Street of Seven Bridges'.

Under the Romans

Over the following centuries, through warfare and cultural absorption, Etruria gradually became part of the **Roman Republic** (later Empire). The Romans built roads such as the Via Cassia and Via Aurelia and colonized enthusiastically, often on Etruscan sites, to consolidate their rule. **Pisa** became an important naval base; **Siena** and **Florence** were founded (the latter by Julius Caesar as the easiest point to cross the Arno) and settled by army veterans.

Christianity reached Tuscany in the early 2nd century. Meanwhile, the Roman Empire declined and fell. Under **Diocletian** (AD285–305) it was divided into East and West, weakening rather than consolidating its political clout. The Western Empire became prey to **Goths** and **Vandals**, barbarian forces from northern Europe, and in 476 the king of the Goths, **Odoacar**, deposed Emperor Romulus Augustulus, ending the Western Empire. In 568 the **Lombards**, warriors from the Danube valley, established control over much of central Italy and made their headquarters at **Lucca**.

Holy Roman Empire

Although converted to Christianity, the Lombards were unwelcome guests in Italy and the popes enlisted foreign aid to expel them. They were finally ousted by **Charlemagne**, the Frankish king, who was crowned Holy Roman Emperor in 800 by Pope Leo III in return. At first little more than an honorary title, the **Holy Roman Empire** became the focus of constant strife between rival claims of successive popes and emperors.

Rise of the City-States

While Emperor and Pope argued over who should rule, the lack of effective central government enabled many Tuscan cities to experience their first taste of **independence**. Trade and industry prospered; individual towns became richer and more powerful, and also gained control of the surrounding lands. Each city's golden age was accompanied by a **construction boom** and **outpouring of creativity**, still very much in evidence today.

Siena became a republic in the 12th century and its wealth was established by the *popolo grasso*, the bourgeoise money-lenders. Involved in a constant power struggle with Florence for control of the Arno valley, Siena was also for many years subject to foreign control until being ceded to Florence in 1557.

For two centuries **Pisa** had a powerful maritime empire, gaining control of Corsica and Sardinia and establishing footholds in Sicily and the Middle East. The city went into slow decline following its naval defeat by Genoa in 1284, subject to frequent periods of foreign government before submitting to Florence in 1406.

Although **Lucca** lacked access to the sea, business (namely banking and the activities of the silk merchants) flourished and by the 14th century it was second only to Florence. The sole city-state to retain independence from Florence, Lucca was given as a present from Napoleon to his sister, Elisa Baciocchi, in 1805. Only in 1847 did the city become part of Tuscany.

Following the death in 1115 of Countess Matilda, **Florence** became a self-governing community and embarked upon its slow but inexorable domination of the region, beginning with the sack of Fiesole in 1125 and systematically destroying the feudal domains of hostile barons in its hinterland.

Guelfs and Ghibellines

The city-states were riven by constant internal strife and endless rivalry with their neighbours. From the middle of the 13th century the quarrel between emperor and papacy developed into a savage struggle between **Guelfs** (the

---

THE *CONTRADE*

Unique to Siena, the *contrade* is a welfare system dating from the Middle Ages. At the height of its powers Siena was divided into 40 small territories called *contrade* but since the 17th century there have been just 17. Each has a distinctive name and is identified by an animal insignia such as an elephant, goose and so on, and a brightly coloured banner. Babies are baptized into the *contrada*: allegiance is for life but support can be expected from the *contrada* during times of need. Each *contrada* has a social club, museum, church and fountain. Ten of the *contrade* are selected to take part in the Palio festivals of 2 July and 16 August, when rivalry often flares into violence.

WHAT'S IN A NAME?

The name 'Guelf' originates from the Welf family, who supported the papacy. In Florence the Guelfs were further divided into the Neri (Blacks) and Bianchi (Whites) following a feud between two branches of one family. Florentine families took opposite sides and the quarrel led to the exile of Dante from Florence in 1302 when the city was purged of the Whites. 'Ghibelline' may originate from Waiblingen, the name of an estate belonging to the Holy Roman Emperors, or from their battle cry of 'Hie Weibling'. Long after they lost their original significance, the Guelf and Ghibelline labels were used for just about every difference of opinion, and some claim they still influence Tuscan politics today.

papal side) and **Ghibellines** (imperial supporters), a battle for territory and political power that divided communities and cities throughout central Italy. In general, the new middle class of merchants and artisans allied with the Guelfs; the old feudal aristocracy hoped to hold democracy in check by allying with the Emperor's Ghibelline faction. Powerful families satisfying personal vendettas caused further splits. There were no decisive victories and new alliances were constantly created. On the whole, the wealthy middle classes were in the ascent, particularly in Florence.

Florence and the Renaissance

Despite factionalism, in-fighting, and general political instability, Florence continued to prosper, accumulating a vast fortune mostly through the **wool trade** and the rise of **money-lending**. By the 14th century, Florence was one of the richest cities in Europe, able to withstand the **banking crisis** precipitated by the English king Edward III's reneging on his debts and the devasting effects of the **Black Death** which decimated the population. The republic also expanded territorially, winning **Arezzo** (1384) and **Pisa** (1406), which gave the city direct access to the sea.

The new-found opulence paved the way for investment in architecture and art on a major scale which blossomed into the **Italian Renaissance** and lasted for more than 200 years. Public displays of **patronage** brought prestige and power. Initially, artistic patronage lay in the hands of the **merchant guilds** (*arti*) who dominated Florentine politics during the 14th century – the wool merchants, for example,

Left: *One of Brunelleschi's last, and most successful, projects – the Pazzi Chapel in Florence.*
Opposite: *Renovated for Lorenzo the Magnificent and remodelled during the 19th century, the Villa Medici at Poggio a Caiano is open to the public.*

were responsible for the building and decoration of Florence's **cathedral**. However, the backlash following the *Ciompi* revolt (*see* panel, this page) broke the power of the guilds in favour of an **oligarchy** of wealthy families, of whom the **Medici** were to become pre-eminent.

The Medici

In a sense 1434, the year **Cosimo de Medici** returned from exile, is the time when Medici rule in Florence began, but it is a great mistake to suppose that Florence ceased to be a republic at this time. Although Cosimo's long period of power established the Medici and enabled the family to dominate Florentine and Tuscan politics for several centuries, there were also interludes when the Medici were exiled, notably 1494–1512 and again in 1527. Cosimo worked behind the scenes as the leader of an influential group, not a ruler – his power was based on the fact that he was widely supported and financially influential (he used crippling tax assessments as a weapon against his enemies and sent many into exile). His grandson, **Lorenzo il Magnifico**, Lorenzo the Magnificent, increased his security following the failure of the 1478 **Pazzi conspiracy** (an assassination plot against him) by hanging more than 300 of his enemies.

Meanwhile, as the Italian Renaissance spread out across Europe, Italy became a **battleground** in which France and Spain both tried to establish hegemony.

THE GUILD SYSTEM

The guilds were originally formed to protect the interests of Florence's commercial classes. The council of Florence was composed of members elected from the city's guilds, appointed for a fixed term, but some guilds were much more influential than others. For a long time the power of the guilds enabled Florence to avoid despotism and remain a republic, but it was far from democratic. In 1378 the *Ciompi*, the lowest paid of the wool workers, rebelled, demanding the right to form their own guild and be represented on the council. After initial victory the movement failed for lack of support among the humbler guilds.

Charles VII of France invaded Italy in 1494 and from then on Italy lacked political autonomy until unification nearly 400 years later.

Medici rule hardened into **autocracy** when **Cosimo I** became Grand Duke of Tuscany in 1570, an event which also confirmed Florentine control over Tuscany. The dynasty lasted for another two centuries until the death of Anna Maria Medici in 1737, when Tuscany was inherited by the Hapsburgs and became part of the **Austro-Hungarian Empire**.

Towards Unification

In 1798 **Napoleon Bonaparte** invaded Tuscany and created the kingdom of **Etruria**. Following Napoleon's downfall in 1815 the Hapsburgs returned, but a home-grown desire for Italian unification (known as the *Risorgimento*) arose, fostered by secret societies such as the Carbonari and Young Italy.

For many centuries Italy had been regarded as the part of Europe least likely to be united and seemed to deserve Metternich's observation that it was merely 'a geographical expression'. However, in 1848 **political unrest** swept through the Italian peninsula. The ultimate failure of the 1848 revolutions proved that the expulsion of foreigners required consummate diplomatic and military skills. These talents were provided by Count

---

THE MEDICI DYNASTY

The Medici, an old Florentine family whose fortune accrued through banking, dominate the history of Renaissance Florence. The family's most illustrious scions were **Cosimo the Elder** (1434–64) and his grandson **Lorenzo the Magnificent** (1469–92). Cosimo in particular sym-bolized the Renaissance ideal of the 'universal man': a successful businessman, astute politician, intellectual and patron of the arts. Lorenzo was a well-respected humanist scholar and poet, who presided over the artistic achievements of luminaries such as Michelangelo and Leonardo da Vinci, but was a less able businessman: the Medici bank failed just before his death and the power of the Medici family was temporarily eclipsed.

Camillo di Cavour and Giuseppe Garibaldi (*see* panel, page 18). The role of Cavour was entirely diplomatic; Garibaldi was the first-rate guerilla chief who proved that Italy could make it herself – without foreign aid. Between them they finally achieved the **unification of Italy** under the House of Piedmont in 1861. Florence was capital of the new kingdom until 1871, when Rome became the capital of a united Italy. The history of Tuscany has since largely been part of the story of modern Italy.

The Twentieth Century

Italian nationalism soured after World War I and in 1922 the fascist leader, **Mussolini**, marched on Rome and assumed power. In Tuscany, towns divided into fascist and anti-fascist factions much along the same lines as Guelfs and Ghibellines. Mussolini took Italy into World War II in 1940 as an ally of Hitler. In Florence all the bridges except the Ponte Vecchio were blown up by the Germans and the city was **occupied** by the Allies in 1944.

Mussolini was executed in 1945 while trying to flee to Switzerland and the monarchy was briefly restored. However, in 1946 the **Republic** was re-proclaimed by a popular referendum and Umberto II and his family were exiled and took up residence in Switzerland. In 1957, Italy became one of the six founder members of the **European Common Market**, now known as the European Union, by signing the Treaty of Rome.

In 1966 the River Arno burst its banks and **flooded** Florence, damaging the city's buildings and works of art so severely that reconstruction and restoration took several decades to complete. The 1993 Mafia **bomb** at the Uffizi Gallery shocked the world, but to date there have fortunately been no repeat performances.

Opposite: *The city of Pisa, like Florence, grew up around the Arno.* **Below:** *Italy gained its independence in 1861.*

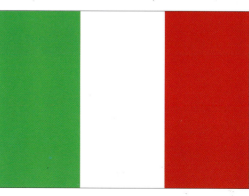

CAVOUR AND GARIBALDI

Count Camillo di Cavour (1810–61) and Giuseppe Garibaldi (1807–82) were poles apart. Cavour was an aristocrat, Garibaldi the son of a merchant seaman. Cavour, described by Mazzini as 'the pale ghost of Machiavelli', was a parliamentarian who opposed revolution and radicalism. Garibaldi was an ill-educated sailor, guerilla leader, a populist and true radical. Cavour wanted an enlarged Piedmont, Garibaldi insisted that a single Italy must be the first goal. Cavour said of Garibaldi: 'Behind his outward petulance there lies the profound dissimulation of a savage'. Garibaldi considered Cavour 'a low intriguer'.

Below: *Freedom fighter Garibaldi meets King Vittorio Emanuele II. This statue stands in Fiesole.*

GOVERNMENT AND ECONOMY

The region of Tuscany comprises 10 provinces, namely Florence, Pistoia, Prato, Pisa, Massa-Carrara, Lucca, Livorno, Grosseto, Siena and Arezzo. Despite a history of autonomy, this area is governed from Rome and has been for some 140 years, like other regions of the republic of Italy.

The country has a ceremonial head of state, the president, who is elected for seven years by the parliament and regional representatives. It is he who nominates the prime minister. Parliament has two chambers – 630 members of the **Chamber of Deputies** and 315 members of the **Senate**. In addition, there are five life members nominated by the current and previous presidents. Despite being governed from Rome, a number of towns and provinces do, however, group together under a Tuscan banner to promote commercial and tourism exploits.

Five hundred years ago cloth, banking, stone and agriculture were mainstays of the economy. Today, the economy is kept afloat by Tuscany's **tourism** (over seven million tourists visit Florence annually), viticulture, agriculture, the marble and stone industries (around Carrara), fabric mills, clothing manufacture, the leather industry, shipbuilding (Livorno), iron ore (Elba) and

general light industry. The most industrial areas are to be found around Prato, Livorno and Arezzo, and in those towns around Florence, such as Sesto Fiorentino and Scandicci, which have now become indistinguishable from the larger city's suburbs.

THE PEOPLE
Language

Italian is the lingua franca of Italy and, it is said, at its purest in Florence. The Florentines have their own dialect – but to the passing tourist, it will probably sound much the same. Thanks to centuries of diplomatic exchange, and now television and the Internet, the urban Tuscans have picked up foreign language

skills. For the tourist whose vocabulary is limited to a simple *buon giorno*, *grazie* and *ciao*, there will be little problem in communication for the Tuscans will want to practice their language skills.

Above: *Cycling tourists are encouraged to explore the Tuscan back roads.*

Religion

Roman Catholicism has always had a strong foothold in Tuscany and as you wander through the region's myriad churches and cathedrals, the various orders will start to distinguish themselves. Benedictine, Cicstercian, Dominican, Franciscan, Carthusian and Carmelites form the backbone of the religious community.

Although the Catholic clergy has reduced in number over the centuries, and the Church in influence, they are still present but gather smaller congregations (and fewer wealthy patrons). Many churches are having difficulty in making ends meet and in some places not only are they only open for a short period daily but there may be an entrance fee to see artistic treasures.

For the sizeable non-Catholic population there is a choice between Protestant churches in Florence, Siena and Lucca, while both Florence and Siena have well-patronized synagogues.

Festivals

The annual festivals that marked the Medieval calendar have, in many towns, withstood the passage of years. Complete with period costumes, caparisoned horses and robust carousing, these events have not just survived but, thanks also to tourism, are even thriving.

Top of the list must be Siena's **Palio** (2 July and 16 August), then Florence's **Scoppio del Caro** (Easter Sunday), **Maggio Musicale** (May), **Calcio Storico** (end June) and **Rificolona** (lantern festival, September), Arezzo's **Giostra del Saracino**, (end August, beginning September), Montalcino's **Sagra del Tordo** (a costumed pageant and ball, last Sunday in October) Pisa's **Regattas** (June), **Luminara** (a lantern festival to celebrate patron saint, San Ranieri, on 16 June) and the **Gioco del Ponte** (an ancient mock battle for control of Ponte di Mezzo). Pistoia's **Giostro dell'Orso** (Bear Joust, July), Impruneta's **Grape Festival** (harvest festival, third week in October); Prato's **Il Sacro Cingalo** (the presentation of the Holy Girdle, various times in the year) and Viareggio's **Carnavale** (processions and floats on Shrove Tuesday).

Fine Art

Tuscan art starts with the Etruscans, a highly talented civilization that inhabited Tuscany between the 8th and 2nd centuries BC. Their legacy includes bronze urns, statues and **funerary items** which can be seen in museums such as Volterra's **Museo Etrusco Guarnacci**.

The **Romans** came and conquered Etruria, but little remains of them. At the turn of the second millennium, religious orders began asserting their differences and constructing new monasteries and churches. Some beautiful examples of **Romanesque** architecture still exist though many Romanesque buildings were finished or modified later, in the subsequent Gothic style imported from northern Europe.

From the late Middle Ages, an increase in **mercantile wealth** led to another wave of **religious construction**. The local guilds were particularly strong and undertook many new building projects. The three most affluent business centres in the region, namely Pisa, Siena and Florence, became trendsetters and each town developed its own artistic style.

Pisa traded with the Orient and its architecture reflects this influence. The impressive **cathedral**, **baptistry** and **campanile** are all tributes to its own style incorporating Byzantine elements and geometric decoration. **Siena** looked northwards and adopted the Gothic lines – pointed arches, accent on the vertical, and single naves – but went little further with exploring its possibilities.

It was in **Florence** that the changes were not influenced by neighbours or trading partners, but by the past in order to move art forward.

By the late 13th century, **Ancient Rome** had been rediscovered. Artists were ripe for a new perception offering a window onto the real world, for a three-dimensionality, a simplification of style and even new subject matter – religious works were, until this time, the norm. In their quest for new expression, they experimented with various media, often mastering a range of disciplines. The once humble craftsman now acquired not only new skills, but a new and dignified status in society.

Giotto (1266–1337) was the first artist to be accorded such due status. A master of fresco painting

---

BRUNELLESCHI (1377–1446)

Filippo Brunelleschi trained as a goldsmith and sculptor in Florence. His contributions to art lay in his understanding and use of perspective to create the illusion of distance, in both architecture and in painting. Among his works are the **Foundlings Hospital** (an early architectural commission dating from 1421), the **Duomo**, **Santo Spirito**, **San Lorenzo**, and the **Pazzi Chapel**, Florence. In 1433 he spent some time in Rome and came back to Florence with renewed ideas about classical architecture.

Opposite: *A calendar of colourful festivals enlivens a visit to the region.*
Below: *Pisa's Baptistry is one of the city's loveliest architectural gems.*

GETTING TO GRIPS WITH THE CENTURIES

In English we talk of the 1300s, the 1400s, the 1500s or the 1600s. In Italian these centuries are known as *trecento, quattrocento, cinquecento* and *seicento*. The Renaissance began in the early *quattrocento*, reached its height in the late *quattrocento* and early *cinquecento*, while Medieval art is *trecento* and, on rarer occasions, *duecento*, from the 1200s. This system continues up to the *novecento*, the 1900s, falling short of our present era, which is *contemporaneo*.

Below: *Michelangelo's* Holy Family, *painted for the Doni family.*

who saw traditional scenes with new eyes, he was charged with overseeing the rebuilding of **Florence Cathedral**. He was chosen not for his architectural record, but because he was a fine forward-thinking painter, with a reputation in the arts.

By the 1400s, the new nobles of Florence (led by the powerful **Medici family**) saw the many advantages of patronage and began sponsoring the building of chapels and charitable foundations. Such commissions benefitted both patron and public, and the new breed of talented artists was much in demand.

Among the innovators was **Brunelleschi (1377–1446)**. He started out as a goldsmith and sculptor but turned his hand to architecture, having studied perspective and Roman buildings, and became one of the founding fathers of the **Renaissance**. In his wake, **Michelozzo (1396–1472)** became Cosimo the Elder's favourite architect, while **Giuliano da Sangallo (1443–1516)** and the great **Michelangelo (1475–1564)** were to continue the trend for later Medicis. **Leone Battista Alberti (1404–72)** studied classical remains in Rome, wrote a treatise on architecture and tried to adapt Roman civic architecture to religious and domestic uses.

Representing the plastic arts, **Nicola** (ca. 1220–84) and **Giovanni Pisano** (ca. 1245–1314), father and son sculptors, earned reputations in Pisa bringing alive the ornate Romanesque style on the **pulpit** in the cathedral. They worked also in Siena: many a figure on the façade was Giovanni's. Their artistic successor in Siena was **Jacopo della Quercia (1371–1438)**, a talented local sculptor. Sculptor **Lorenzo Ghiberti (1378–1455)** broke all preconceived moulds when he created Florence cathedral's **North Doors**.

It was left to young **Donatello** (ca. 1385–1466), a highly innovative artist, to move sculpture forward again with a hitherto unseen force and realism. He influenced much of later Florentine sculpture and, until **Michelangelo** (*see* panel, page 47), no-one came near him in talent.

In the field of religious painting, **Giotto** left an influential legacy in his **Santa Croce** frescoes and in **Arezzo**. When **Masaccio** (1401–28) frescoed part of the **Brancacci Chapel** and created Santa Maria Novella's *Holy Trinity with Virgin, St John and Donors*, painting took another great leap forward. Here he shows that he had mastered lessons of perspective, the depiction of human emotion and use of light for modelling. Along with two of his friends, Brunelleschi and Donatello, Masaccio formed the triumvirate which led the way to the **Renaissance**.

Following in Masaccio's footsteps (and, according to chronicler **Vasari**, everyone studied his work) came the less innovative but now popular **Paolo Uccello** (ca. 1396–1475) whose subjects showed his preoccupation with perspective; and the great masters of fresco, **Fra Angelico** (1400–55), who grasped the concept of perspective, but clung to soft, gentle colours and images to convey a certain purety of spirit; **Ghirlandaio** (1449–94); the talented **Fra Filippo Lippi** (1406–69); and his son, **Filippino** (ca. 1457–1504).

Ghirlandaio taught **Michelangelo** for a short period (*see* panel, page 47), while his son, Ridolfo, was a friend of Raphael's and had a distinguished career as a portrait painter; Filippo taught his own son and **Sandro Botticelli** (1445–1510), who rose to be one of the great individuals in the Renaissance (many of his works are displayed in the **Uffizi**).

In the mid-15th century other notable artists were in great demand. These included **Piero della Francesca** (1416–92), who worked in Borgo Sansepolcro and Arezzo; his pupil, **Luca Signorelli** (ca. 1441–1523); and **Perugino** (1446–1523), possibly a pupil of Piero and a contemporary of Leonardo.

Above: *Renaissance man, Leonardo da Vinci.*

TERMINOLOGY IN ART

Abbazia • abbey
Badia • abbey
Basilica • a church or cathedral with nave, no separate aisles
Cappella • chapel
Cenacolo • both a refectory and a painting of the Last Supper
Chiesa • church
Cupola • dome
Duomo • cathedral
Eremito • hermitage
Fresco • a wall painting, executed in wet plaster
Intarsia • inlaid work in stone, wood or metal
Opera • artistic work
Pieve • parish church
Putto • small cherub or angel, often nearly nude
Tondo • round painting or low-relief sculpture

DANTE ALIGHIERI

Dante Alighieri was born in Florence to minor nobility and White Guelf sympathizers. With Guido Cavalacanti he formed a movement called the *Dolce Stil Nuovo*, Sweet New Style. As a young adult he fell in love with the even younger **Beatrice Portinari**. His interest in politics started in his early twenties, and by 1300 he became Florentine representative to the Pope. But the Black Guelfs rose against the White Guelfs and Dante was thrown out of public office and condemned to death. His sentence was later commuted to exile, and in 1302 he left Florence, never to return. In later years he saw his distance from Florence as a distance from corruption. It was during his exile that he wrote the masterpieces, the *Divine Comedy* and the *Monarchy*. He died in Ravenna at the age of 56.

Out on a limb, and destined to move art into the High Renaissance, **Leonardo da Vinci** (1452–1519) also studied with **Perugino** under goldsmith, sculptor and painter, **Verrocchio** (1435–88) and soon set out on his own (*see panel, page 65*).

In the provinces young Raffaello Sanzio (**Raphael**, 1483–1520) worked with Perugino as an adolescent, and at the age of 17 received his first commission. He was the second of the three great creators of the **High Renaissance** and his works are displayed in the Pitti Palace. His contemporary, though not his equal, **Sodoma** (1477–1549) was a sought-after artist in Siena while fellow Sienese, **Domenico Beccafumi** (ca. 1484–1551), moved Sienese art towards the rather contrived, rule-breaking, Mannerist movement.

With the rise of Mannerism and the Baroque, Rome assumed premier position in the patronage of the arts.

Literature, Music and Cinema

Its was perhaps no coincidence that three of Italy's finest writers – Boccaccio, Petrarch and Dante – were all Tuscan and born at a time when most writing was still in Latin. Then **Dante Alighieri** (1265–1321) began a movement to write in the vernacular, thereby sounding the death knell for Latin, except in Church. His most famous work is the allegorical poem, *Divine Comedy*, which still makes good reading. So too does **Giovanni Boccaccio's** (1313–75) *Decameron*.

The earthiness of Boccaccio's work contrasts with the elegance of that of **Francesco Petrarch** (1304–74), one of Italy's greatest poets, and crowned *Prince of Poets*. Another famous name is that of politician **Niccolò Machiavelli** (1469–1527). Surrounded by creative thinkers, **Lorenzo the Magnificent** tried his hand at poetry. The great artists (**Alberti**, **Leonardo**, **Michelangelo**, **Piero della Francesca**, **Vasari**) also turned their skills to treatise writing. Another important personality was **Galileo Galilei**

(1564–1642), the Pisa-born mathematician. It was, in retrospect, a golden age of Tuscan literature, for little of note appeared for nearly two centuries until *Pinocchio* raised his wooden head, thanks to **Carlo Lorenzini** (1826–90).

In terms of music, there have been considerably fewer local notables. **Giacomo Puccini** (1858–1924) is probably the best known Tuscan, though many forget that **Gian Battista Lully** (1632–87) was born in Florence.

As with music, Tuscany has not given birth to very many great film directors. The **Taviani Brothers** from San Miniato are the exception. Their best known films are *La Notte di San Lorenzo* and *Good Morning Babilonia*. When it comes to scenery, however, Tuscany has been used in many films, such as **Merchant Ivory's** adaptation of *Room with a View* and **Kenneth Branagh's** adaptation of Shakespeare's *Much Ado about Nothing*. Glimpses of Tuscany can also be gleaned in film adaptations such as **Jane Campion's** *Portrait of a Lady*, **Anthony Mingella's** *The English Patient*, **Roberto Begnini's** *La Vita è Bella* and even **Ridley Scott's** *Gladiator*.

> **FAMOUS FOREIGNERS IN TUSCANY**
>
> Lured by its cultural environment, a number of English and American writers chose either to visit or to live for long periods in Tuscany. These include:
> **Bernard Berenson**, art historian, Florence;
> **EM Forster**, writer, Florence;
> **Aldous Huxley**, writer, Viareggio;
> **DH Lawrence**, writer, Florence and Tuscany;
> **Elizabeth Barrett Browning**, writer, Florence;
> **Henry James**, novelist, Florence;
> **John Ruskin**, art critic, Lucca;
> **Percy Bysshe Shelley**, poet, Pisa.

Sports

Following the practice of earlier times, there are annual tournaments, **jousts** and **football** games when traditionally one town district is pitted against another. Instead of sporting shorts and T-shirts, the players are kitted out in Medieval dress which in some cases include armoury. These are great spectator sports, as they have been for 500 years and more.

Other sports loved by Tuscans include **football** (Florence's Fiorentina is a premier team), **rowing** (the Arno is a popular spot for the rowing clubs) and **water sports**. Beaches such as Marina di Carrara, Punta Ala and those on Elba have good facilities for **sailing**, **windsurfing**, **canoeing**, and **swimming**. **Cycling** enthusiasts

Opposite: *An engaging interpretation of Carlo Lorenzini's* Pinocchio.
Below: *Rowing is a popular pastime on the River Arno.*

Opposite: *Tuscany excels in its fresh market produce.*
Below: *With the first rays of warm sun, a Pienza café spills onto the street.*

might want to get hold of *Discovering Tuscany by Bike*, from the Tuscan Regional Tourist Office, as it offers various itineraries for cyclists. In winter, **skiers** head for Abetone where there are also ice-skating facilities.

Food and Drink

Although the French might disagree, the Tuscans consider their cuisine amongst the world's finest. The region produces **excellent ingredients**: fresh fruit and vegetables, meat and fish. Combined with its fragrant herbs and some of the country's rich **olive oils**, its best wines and a small *digestif*, this can add up to a simple and delicious cuisine.

Once at table and after ordering from an à la carte menu, the waiter may well bring something to nibble on while waiting – *crostini*, small slices of baguette-type bread spread with liver pâté, *bruschetta*, large slices of bread rubbed in oil and salt, *grissini*, breadsticks, and slices of salt-free country bread.

The *primo piatto*, or first course, can take various forms. A *minestra*, soup, is a warm welcome in winter; try for instance the famous *acquacotta*, a bouillon vegetable soup with an egg on top, or *ribollita*, a well-stewed vegetable and bean soup. *Antipasto Mixto*, mixed cold hors d'œuvres, is another favourite and might include cooked artichoke, Parma ham, salami, cooked mushrooms and sometimes cooked seafood.

The **pasta course** (in smart restaurants you have both *antipasto* and pasta) will comprise plenty of familiar pastas. But it will also include *polenta*, originally a cornmeal staple of the poor – an acquired taste. It is the **sauces** that change. There are always *ragù*, *bolognese*, minced meat with tomatoes, butter and sage sauces, basil-loaded pestos, and plain tomato, but try the *ragù de lepre*, made from hare and usually served with *pappardelle*, broad ribbon pasta; sauces made with cream and *rucola*, rocket; with *porcini* mushrooms or with *tartufo* (truffle – expensive but delicious). There is usually lasagna too.

When it comes to the *secondo piatto*, or main dish, there is nothing finer for the meat lover than the famous *bistecca alla Fiorentina*, a doorstep of rump steak, often grilled over an open fire, which should be prepared with Val di Chiana beef. Alternatively, *stracotto*, beef simmered in red wine, is excellent. *Vitello*, veal, comes in many guises: cold with a tuna sauce (odd but good), *scaloppine*, scallops, or *testina di vitello*, cooked veal head. *Agnello*, lamb, is particularly popular in spring while *lepre*, hare, *cinghiale*, boar, and other game are served in winter. Tripe and *coniglio*, rabbit, are served year-round, while poultry lovers should try *faraone*, guinea fowl, or *quaglia*, quail. *Pesce*, fish, and *frutta di mare*, seafood, though expensive, are both popular on the coast where nothing beats the delicious *fritto misto*, a light, easily digested presentation of mixed fried seafoods. Also look out for *tonno*, tuna, *pesce spada*, swordfish, and *sogliola*, sole, on menus.

Meat dishes are never served with **vegetables** – this comes extra: *spinaci*, spinach, *finocchi*, artichoke, *melanzane*, eggplant, *peperoni*, bell peppers, *fagioli*, white beans, or *fagiolini*, green string beans, and, in season, *fiori di zucchini*, courgette flowers, or *piselli*, peas. *Insalata mista*, mixed salad, is available everywhere.

Tuscany produces a few *formaggi*, cheeses, and perhaps its *pecorino* is the best of the lot. A mature sheep's

VIRGIN OR EXTRA VIRGIN?

Fruit of Athena's olive tree, rich, nutritious and simply delicious, olive oil is the staple of Tuscany's cuisine. It is said that the best oil of all, extra virgin, naturally, comes from around **Lucca**. Needing little attention except annual pruning and weeding, the harvest swings into action around All Saints' Day, 1 November.

The first, cold pressing from the newly picked olives, using a traditional millstone, produces the best oil with the lowest acidity – extra virgin oil has less than one per cent. It is thick, green and highly perfumed. Subsequent pressings, or pressings with more acid fruit, produce an oil which carries the simple description: virgin olive oil. Italy produces some 24 per cent of world output, and oils from Tuscany are consistently among the most prized and, therefore, on the expensive side.

Above: *Vineyards cloak many of the Tuscan hills.*
Opposite: *Chianti is Tuscany's favourite wine.*

milk cheese (sometimes with a percentage of cow's milk) it is served alone, on pasta, with pears or apples and is quite delicious.

Desserts are not Italy's forte but you will find *tiramisù*, that creamy mascarpone, sponge and liquor confection that has travelled well beyond Italy's borders, and often baked and caramelized fruits. Siena produces *panforte*, a rich fruit cake, Perugia is known for its *panettone*, a lighter-than-light sponge cake, and everywhere there are seasonal fruits which, in summer, can include figs, peaches, nectarines, strawberries (often with lemon juice), cherries and apricots. Alternatively, a Tuscan favourite is to take a glass of *vino santo*, a fine dessert wine somewhere between port and sherry. Enjoy it with *cantucci*, small, dry and very hard biscuits made with almonds which, when dipped in the wine, soften and melt in the mouth. As a parting thought, Perugia is known for its *Baci di Perugia*, or 'Perugian kisses' – a fine name for small chocolates.

Stepping aside from fine cuisine, Tuscany also produces many a good **pizza**. Cooked in wood-fire ovens, they are a simple and filling alternative to *alta cucina*.

Wines and Spirits

The **wine** industry in Italy has expanded beyond all imagination in the last 30 years when the familiar Chianti bottle, the *fiasco*, was practically all anyone knew of Tuscan wine. There were even better wines, but they rarely left the country. Today, the **DOC** (*Denominazione d'Origine Controllata*, the system of controlling the origin and the vinification of wine) and the superior **DOCG** (which adds that the quality is guaranteed) systems ensure a consistently good wine and the choice is vast

COFFEE OR CAFFÈ?

The most common cup of coffee is the ***espresso***, quick, short, and strong, usually drunk standing at the bar. If you fancy just a dash of milk, ask for a ***caffè macchiato***. A ***caffè corretto*** is a coffee with a tot of grappa spirit. The ***cappuccino*** is an espresso, topped by frothy milk and dusted off with chocolate powder. An alternative to this is the ***caffè latte***, milky coffee without the froth. If you want a coffee that's half milk, half coffee, try asking for ***caffè lungo con latte*** which may well be served in a glass. Coffee drunk in the States, a far weaker brew, is called ***caffè Americano*** and is often made with instant coffee.

(*see* panel, page 67). If you don't want to order a full bottle of wine, ask for *vino della casa*, house wine, which is usually sold by the quarter, half or litre.

Among the region's best wines are still its **Chianti Classico**, controlled more rigidly than before and therefore of a higher quality than that from the Sienese and Florentine vineyards on the slopes of the Chianti hills; **Brunello di Montalcino** is one of the country's most reputed red wines and improves with ageing; **Vernaccia**, from San Gimignano, is a pale, dry wine; another white wine is the delicate **Bianco di Pitigliano**. Back with the reds, the **Nobile di Montepulciano** is also an excellent wine, and one for laying down.

Elba produces a rich, ruby-coloured **Dolce Aleatico**, a sweet red dessert wine, while the region's much loved *vino santo*, a straw-coloured or deep amber-hued dessert wine, is particularly appreciated from the Chianti Classico and Montepulciano areas.

Italy is also renowned for a number of apéritifs and *digestifs* which are excellent. Top of the list are the apéritif brands **Campari**, **Cinzano** and **Martini**, while *digestifs* **Fernet Branca**, made from herbs, *grappa*, a spirit made from grape must, *amaretto*, an almond flavoured *digestif*, and *sambuca*, an aniseed liqueur, are all popular. At party time, Italy's answer to champagne, *prosecco* (remember **Asti Spumante**?), brings a bit of bubble to the occasion.

Beer lovers have a choice between **Peroni**, **Nastro Azzuro** and **Moretti** which will probably be served *alla spina* (draught) in the bar.

Lastly, although tap water is perfectly safe, most Italians prefer bottled **mineral water**. Ferrarelle, San Pellegrino and San Benedetto are popular *frizzante*, sparkling waters.

EVOLUTION OF CHIANTI WINE

It is possible that wine has been grown in the Chianti region for over 2500 years. The modern industry owes its roots to Bettino Ricasoli, marquis and wine maker in the 1800s, who set down guidelines for its content, vinification and geographical area of production. Chianti's name was not a synonym for fine wine until the late 20th century when a huge change took place in the expansion of vine-producing land and the regulation of the industry. True Chianti (which may also encompass sub-areas such as Chianti Ruffina, Chianti Colli Fiorentini or Chianti Colli Aretini) carries the *DOC* label. It is produced from the red Sangiovese grape, with the addition of small quantities of red Canaiolo, Trebbiano (a white grape) and other varieties. The region in which Chianti wine may be produced covers over 100 *comuni*, from Pistoia in the north to Montalcino in the south, Arezzo in the east, and nearly to Livorno in the west.

2
Florence

One of Europe's small but great cities, Florence has had an influence well beyond the borders of hilly Tuscany. Today it is a living museum where the best Medieval and Renaissance buildings, many of which are beautifully decorated, have been carefully preserved. The city is a showcase of good taste, a monument to its 700-year history and a lesson in fine arts, but a lesson which can be absorbed without study, for its merits are omnipresent and a stroll through town is as edifying as any text book.

The first stop must be the **Duomo**, Florence's most familiar landmark and a sight which seems to provide a backdrop for every city view. Then there are the **churches** and **chapels**, testament to the ecomonic success of the city in the 1300–1500s and the patronage by such wealthy banking families as the Pazzi, the Pitti and the enormously influential Medici, who later became the Grand Dukes of Tuscany; lastly one should visit the **galleries** and noble **palaces** which have accumulated sculpture, painting and decorative arts attesting to man's interest in his past, his quest for pictorial realism and his increasing interest in portraying things secular.

Although Florence is a step into the past for the traveller, any visit to this wonderful city is also enlivened by the many beautiful **shops**, fine **restaurants** and **cafés** which fuel the discovery. For the Florentine, however, whose sights are set not on the past but on the future, the city is a pool of inspiration and a challenge to contemporary artistic talent.

DON'T MISS

*** **The Duomo:** magnificent landmark Cathedral, its Baptistry and Campanile.
*** **Palazzo del Bargello:** a Medieval palace with Italy's greatest sculpture collection.
*** **The Uffizi Gallery:** the greatest Italian Renaissance paintings, under one roof.
*** **Palazzo Pitti:** fabulous museums, and the delightful Boboli Garden.
** **Ponte Vecchio:** best seen as the sun sets over the Arno.
** **Brancacci Chapel:** Masaccio's fresco cycle.
* **Piazzale Michelangelo:** panoramic views of Florence.

Opposite: *Detail from Santa Maria del Fiore in Florence.*

PIAZZA DEL DUOMO

The heart of the Tuscan world, the centre of Medieval Florence and home to the buildings which revolutionized the future of art and architecture, Piazza del Duomo is where you start any discovery of this magical city.

Duomo ***

The exterior of this imposing cathedral, dedicated to **Santa Maria del Fiore**, is beautiful (the interior, by contrast, is rather plain) but its cupola is magnificent. It is one of Christendom's largest cathedrals, as befitted the rising economic and cultural wealth of Medieval Florence, and is capped by a spectacular dome with an equally spectacular

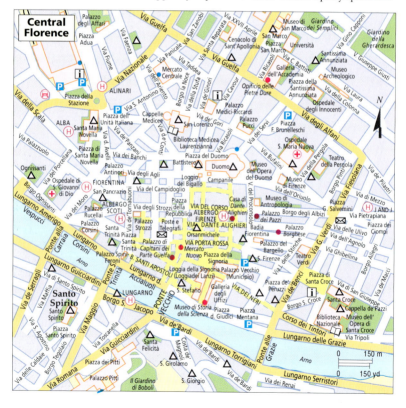

view once the 460-odd wearing steps have been climbed. It was **Arnolfo di Cambio** (ca. 1245–1302) who accepted the prestigious commission and it is his Gothic design we see today, though the red-roofed dome, designed in 1433 to cover the huge sanctuary, was the work of ground-breaking architect **Brunelleschi**. He conceived his sectioned dome much like an egg, with a smaller inner layer and a solid outer layer, with supports between the two. Between these architects, painter **Giotto** was nominated Master of Works by the Medici, who sought to have a 'famous name' in charge, rather than a trained but unknown overseer.

The west façade, originally designed by di Cambio, was reclad in the now familiar green, russet and white marbles during the 19th century.

Above: *Matching marbles were used for the Duomo and the Campanile.*

Battistero (Baptistry) ***

Marvellous as the Medieval, octagonal Baptistry of St John may be, it's the doors which draw the crowds. A competition for two pairs of new bronze doors was launched in 1401 (**Andrea Pisano** had executed the first pair in 1330) and anybody who was notable in the art world clamoured to submit designs. It was young sculptor **Lorenzo Ghiberti** (1378–1455) who won the commission and his North Doors, harmonizing well with Pisano's work, show scenes from the *Life of Christ*, the *Evangelists* and the *Doctors of the Church* (with a self-portrait on the frame). But it's the East Doors, the 10 panels of the so-called *Gates of Paradise* (Michelangelo is said to have dubbed them thus) which are truly superb (the originals are in the Museo dell'Opera del Duomo). **Old Testament** scenes unfold with realism and poetry. Save time to admire the glittering *trecento* mosaics inside, with scenes from both Testaments done by Venetian craftsmen.

Campanile **

If you haven't climbed to the top of the Duomo, the view from the top of the Campanile is similar. Designed by **Giotto** in 1334 and clad in coloured marbles, the belfry is probably the most elegant Gothic landmark in Florence.

FLORENCE BY BIKE

Pedestrianized Florence is bike-friendly. There are even a number of bike routes to help ensure cyclists' safety. Currently a pilot scheme (**Mille e Una Bici**, or 1001 Bikes) is underway by the *Comune* of Florence, whereby for a nominal fee of around 1.6 Euros, would-be cyclists can hire a bike from one of the town's 16 main depot/parks. Otherwise, there are two organizations offering bike rental. **Manila Bike**, via Dossio 50, tel: 055 715776, and **Florence by Bike**, via San Zanobia 120r/122r, tel: 055 488992.

Above: *Leather goods in the Mercato Nuovo.*

Museo dell'Opera del Duomo *

Many sculptural items from the Cathedral, Baptistry and Campanile have been moved to this museum (piazza del Duomo 9, open daily), which occupies the same building as the Cathedral Workshop has done since Brunelleschi's day. The highlight is **Michelangelo's** *Pietà* finished by a pupil of his; also works by **Andrea Pisano** and **Giotto**; choral galleries by **Donatello** and **Luca della Robbia**; and the sculptures by **Arnolfo di Cambio** which were crafted for his façade design of the Duomo.

Orsanmichele *

If the architecture of this church appears to be a little unusual, it is because it was originally conceived as a loggia and granary and was designed by **Neri di Fioravanti** and **Francesco Talenti** in the 14th century; then part of it was used as a chapel in the 15th century. It has a pleasant, squarish interior with a fine sculpted, Gothic altarpiece by **Andrea Orcagna** but its major interest lies in the wonderful display of individual statuary which once decorated the external niches (many are copies of originals which have been moved, for protection, either inside or to museums) depicting the patron saints of various Florentine guilds and executed by some of the Renaissance's biggest names. Here were **bronze** statues by **Lorenzo Ghiberti** and **Donatello**, as well as works by **Nanni di Banco**, **Luca della Robbia**, **Bernardo Daddi**, **Simone Talenti**, **Verrocchio** and **Giovanni Tedesco**.

Loggia del Mercato Nuovo *

This 16th-century loggia, on Via Porta Rossa, was built to house the produce market. It now shelters a popular market, also called the **Mercato del Porcellino**, after the bronze fountain in the form of a large boar. Selling straw goods, leather, table linen and souvenirs, it is a big drawcard for tourists.

TREAT YOURSELF IN FLORENCE

Leather gloves: Pusateri, via Calzaiuoli 25r, tel/fax: 055 214192. All colours and styles.
Paper goods: Parione, via Parione 10r, tel/fax: 055 215684. Exquisite cards, booklets and handmade paper.
Perfumes and toiletries: Profumeria Inglese, via de' Tornabuoni 97r, tel: 055 289748. Old-world service.
Leather shoes: Ferragamo, via de' Tornabuoni 2, tel: 055 4395470. Or Antica Cuoieria, via del Corso 48r, tel: 055 2381653. Beautiful shoes.
Luxury foodstuffs: Procacci, via de' Tornabuoni 64r, tel: 055 211656. Truffles and exclusive food produce.
Herbal remedies, toiletries: Erboristeria Inglese, via de' Tornabuoni 19, tel/fax: 055 210628. Atmospheric.
Leather goods: Peruzzi, borgo de' Greci 8–20r, tel: 055 289039. Wide selection.

Piazza della Signoria

Erstwhile centre of civic activity and site of Savonarola's death at the stake in 1498, Piazza della Signoria is still a meeting place for tourists and Florentines alike. The piazza is now dressed with the tables and chairs of smart *caffès* – perfect for people-watching. It also hosts a rather streaky copy of **Michelangelo's** sculpture, *David* (the original is now in the Accademia), which was commissioned for this piazza, a fine **equestrian statue** of Cosimo I by **Giambologna**, and the larger-than-life **Neptune Fountain** by **Ammannati**.

Palazzo Vecchio **

Likewise known by its original name (Palazzo della Signoria), this was the seat of local government, a solid town hall with an elegant tower, probably another work by the cathedral's architect, **Arnolfo di Cambio**. Medici favourite **Michelozzo** was commissioned to redesign parts of the palace in the *quattrocento*, while in the 16th century Cosimo I appropriated it as his residence and called upon **Vasari** to renovate and decorate it to accommodate his luxurious lifestyle.

The Palazzo (open daily) can be visited. Highlights include Vasari's delicate decoration of Michelozzo's **courtyard**, the cavernous **Hall of the 500** decorated by Vasari, the rather claustrophobic but elegant **Studiolo**, once the study of Francesco I (another superb Vasari work), and the extensive **apartments** on the third floor.

Loggia della Signoria **

The fashion for loggias began at the turn of the 13th century. This Gothic one, with rounded arches, was built to shelter civil servants during official ceremonies in the piazza. Sometimes called the **Loggia dei Lanzi**, it houses some exquisite sculpture such as the slightly disturbing *Perseus* (1554) holding up Medusa's severed head, by *cinquecento* goldsmith and sculptor, **Benvenuto Cellini** and the powerful *Rape of the Sabines* (1583) by **Giambologna**.

Below: *Palazzo Vecchio, Piazza della Signoria, with its elegant clock tower.*

MARKETS AROUND TOWN

Open Monday–Saturday only:
Mercato Centrale, Piazza del Mercato Centrale. Florence's best known market under a 19th-century loggia, sprawling into the San Lorenzo area; mornings for fresh veggies, fish, fruit and meat; stalls open all day for leather goods, arty T-shirts, gloves and souvenirs.
Mercato delle Pulci, Piazza dei Ciompi, is the best place to find bric-a-brac, household items and hippy-style clothing.
Mercato Santo Spirito, Piazza Santo Spirito, takes place on the second Sunday of the month, offers bric-a-brac and used clothes, also ethnic items and handcrafted jewellery, pottery, etc.
Mercato Nuovo, Loggia Mercato Nuovo, caters for tourist souvenir requirements.
Mercato delle Cascine, Parco delle Cascine, Viale Lincoln, is further out of town, but better value as its less touristy. It's a real all-round market and includes some clothes.

Palazzo del Bargello ★★★

Severe and uninviting from the exterior, this Medieval palace houses under its Gothic arches a fine collection of decorative arts and one of the best collections of sculpture in Italy, the **Museo Nazionale del Bargello** (via del Proconsolo 4, open mornings, except Wednesday). The building was begun in 1250 when it was crowned with its crenellated tower, and grew through the following century, successively housing political figures, police and prisoners. On entering the elegant courtyard the delightful little **bronze sculpture** of a fisherman by **Vicenzo Gemito**, a 19th-century Neapolitan, is in a prime position.

Among the exhibits in this museum are many early works by **Michelangelo**, including his rather unappealing *Drunk Bacchus* and the *Tondo Pitti*, a round three-dimensional relief destined to be hung on the wall, depicting the Virgin, Child and St John. Don't overlook the *Bust of Cosimo I* (and other works) by **Benvenuto Cellini**, the master goldsmith, sculptor and writer. The works by **Donatello** merit close appreciation. Look at his classical bronze *David*, one of the first Renaissance statues of a nude, and compare it with his much earlier, marble version. Don't miss the *Madonna and Child* by another great and innovative sculptor, **Luca della Robbia**

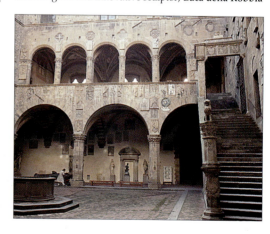

Right: *A fortified palazzo from Medieval times, the Palazzo del Bargello houses one of Italy's most impressive collections of Renaissance sculpture.*

(the uncle of sculptor Andrea and great-uncle of Giovanni della Robbia). This master of glazed terracotta produced a number of delightful semi-three-dimensional sculptures in white, usually on a blue background.

Verrocchio, another leading Renaissance sculptor, is represented by, among others, his slightly contrived *David*. Save some time too for viewing the non-sculptural exhibits in the **Sala Islamica** (carpets, arms), the **Sala degli Avori** (which groups a magnificent collection of ivories) and the items on display in the **Sala Carrand**, a varied collection of artifacts bequeathed to Florence by the Frenchman, Louis Carrand.

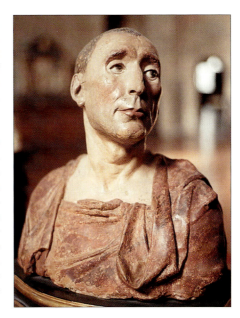

Above: *A new realism hallmarked Renaissance sculpture. Donatello's supposed portrait of Niccolò da Uzzano, in the Museo Nazionale del Bargello, is a good example.*

Badia Fiorentina *

Just opposite the Bargello is the **Badia Fiorentina** – the Benedictine church of an abbey founded in 978, though its Medieval tower was added after 1310, while the church was extensively remodelled in the 17th century. The church's most interesting features are its coffered wooden ceiling and **Filippo Lippi's** *Madonna Appearing to St Bernard*. The church is rarely open, except for the scheduled religious services.

Casa di Dante Alighieri *

Just over the Via del Proconsolo, in Via Dante Alighieri, stands the dignified stone house where Dante (*see* panel, page 24) was supposedly born in 1265. However, chased into exile for his political allegiance in 1302, he never lived here again. Casa di Dante Alighieri is now a **museum** chronicling his life (via Santa Margherita 1, open spring to autumn, daily, except Tuesday). Look at 'Dante's church', just opposite – a small yet tranquil retreat.

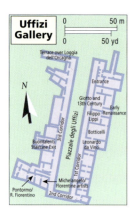

Uffizi Gallery

Above Right: *The Uffizi Gallery backs onto the River Arno.*

GALLERIA DEGLI UFFIZI

Within this large and impressive art gallery (best visited in the late afternoon when it is less crowded) there are some fabulous paintings, many of which will be familiar from reproductions. Mentioned below are a few that merit closer appreciation.

Room 2 houses some early 13th-century works which set the scene for understanding painting at the end of the Middle Ages. There are three interpretations of the *Maestà* by the early masters – **Cimabue**, **Duccio**, and the later painter, **Giotto**.

Room 7 opens onto some familiar sights. A magnificent rendering of the *Virgin and Child with St Anne* by the Gothic painter **Masolino** and his young associate, **Masaccio** (*see* page 42). It shows Masaccio's ability to grasp the concepts of the role light plays in modelling form and dimension. There is also the marvellous profile portrait of *Federico de Montefeltro and Battista Sforza*, the Dukes of Montefeltro, painted in 1472 by **Piero della Francesca** (*see* panel, page 90). The delicate landscapes in the background owe their style more, perhaps, to the Flemish school of painting than the Italian. Nearby is the one large panel from the triptych, *The Battle of San Romano* by **Paolo Uccello**, painted in the mid-15th century for Cosimo the Elder. It is an action-packed battle scene (look how Uccello has created three-dimensional if rather wooden subjects, and how he has mastered foreshortening in the fallen soldier) depicting the Florentine victory over the Sienese in 1432.

Room 8 contains works by **Filippo Lippi** (1406–69), ex-Carmelite monk turned painter who learned from Masaccio and who, in turn, taught his son, Filippino, and Botticelli. His *Virgin and Child with two Saints*, painted in 1464, reflects the sensual nature of this talented painter.

Rooms 10–14, now forming one gallery, are devoted to works by **Sandro Botticelli**. His two famous works, *The Allegory of Spring* and *The Birth of Venus*, are both infinitely more impressive when you stand in front of them than their oft-seen reproductions. The delicacy of brushwork and the fragility of human beauty is captured in a novel way, confirming Botticelli's talent.

Room 15 displays work by **Leonardo da Vinci**, and includes his very early but beautiful *Annunciation* (still influenced by his teacher, Verrocchio) and the unfinished 1481 masterpiece, *Adoration of the Magi*, an illustration of many of the Renaissance's principles of design and form.

Room 25 houses **Michelangelo's** beautiful *tondo* (round painting) of *The Holy Family*, painted for the Doni family in 1504. It was one of his last Florentine commissions – and the only finished painting – before he started work on the Sistine Chapel in Rome.

Room 27 displays, among other fine paintings, **Andrea del Sarto's** powerful 1517 *Madonna of the Harpies*.

Room 28 is home to the gallery's collection of **Titian's** canvases such as the famous reclining *Venus of Urbino*.

> **MORE EXHIBITS AT THE UFFIZI**
>
> Besides artwork from Tuscany, the Uffizi Gallery houses some excellent works by non-Tuscan painters. These include paintings by the Venetians, such as **Titian** with his marvellous nude, ***Venus of Urbino***, and **Paolo Veronese** who painted the ***Holy Family with St Barbara***. There are also paintings by **Giovanni Bellini, Giorgione, Tintoretto** and the later **Canaletto, Longhi** and **Guardi**. The gallery also has works by German **Albrecht Dürer**, Flemish and Dutch artists **Rembrandt, Rubens, Van Dyck** and **Jan Steen**, and even a canvas by Spaniard **Goya**. Lastly, there are also paintings grouped in the collections from which they were donated, as well as collections of ceramics and furniture.

Left: *Sandro Botticelli's* Allegory of Spring *is just one of many highlights in the Uffizi Gallery.*

Below: *Of the nine major bridges spanning the Arno, the Ponte Vecchio is the only pedestrian one.*

Museo di Storia della Scienza *

Adjoining the Uffizi is the Museum of the History of Science, (piazza dei Giudici, 1, open mornings except Sunday; and afternoons, Monday, Wednesday and Friday) housed in the solid, Medieval **Palazzo Castellani**. Dedicated to the evolution of scientific knowledge and scientific instruments, it exhibits many of the instruments made for the Medici Grand Dukes and some of **Galileo's possessions** such as his telescope, compass and, more bizarrely, one of his fingers in a reliquary. The **surgical instruments** provide a parting reflection as to the naïvety and unsophistication of medicine in the Medieval and Renaissance times.

Ponte Vecchio **

Since **Roman times**, this strategic point between north and south banks of the Arno has been linked by a bridge. It is the narrowest part of the river and links the heart of Florence and the Oltrarno. This landmark bridge (the 'Old Bridge') has twice been lashed by the churning waters of the **flooding Arno**. The 1170 bridge was washed away in 1333 and rebuilt in 1345 when butchers and tanners occupied its various shops, making use of the Arno for their waste. So great was the resulting stench that

Grand Duke Ferdinando I evicted them at the end of the 14th century and let the space to jewellers and silversmiths. In the 17th century their workshops were enlarged by cantilevering the floors outwards on wooden poles. During World War II the Ponte Vecchio was the only bridge to be spared in the 1944 raid.

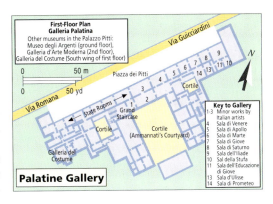

First-Floor Plan
Galleria Palatina
Other museums in the Palazzo Pitti:
Museo degli Argenti (ground floor),
Galleria d'Arte Moderna (2nd floor),
Galleria del Costume (South wing of first floor)

Piazza dei Pitti

Via Guicciardini

Via Romana

State Rooms

Grand Staircase

Cortile

Cortile (Ammannati's Courtyard)

Galleria del Costume

Palatine Gallery

Key to Gallery
1-3 Minor works by Italian artists
4 Sala di Venere
5 Sala di Apollo
6 Sala di Marte
7 Sala di Giove
8 Sala di Saturno
9 Sala dell'Iliade
10 Sal della Stufa
11 Sala dell'Educazione di Giove
13 Sala d'Ulisse
14 Sala di Prometeo

On 4 November 1966, the Arno rose once more and the bridge was yet again under threat. Although some damage was done it was fortunately not irreparable.

The **jewellery tradition** still continues: if you are looking for something typically Florentine, search among the (pricey) shops on the Ponte Vecchio.

PIAZZA DEI PITTI

This large square, uniting **Via Guicciardini** and **Via Romana**, is dominated by the palace of the same name.

Palazzo Pitti ***

One of the largest palaces in Florence, though not necessarily one of the most beautiful, the Pitti Palace now houses a number of interesting museums. The palace was started in 1458 for **Luca Pitti**, a powerful merchant and banker, though it later passed into Medici hands and was converted by Ammannati, providing the family and its heirs with a residence for more than 300 years. During the centuries, the gardens and two wings were added.

The palace houses five museums. Most spectacular is the **Galleria Palatina** (open daily, except Monday, till late). Amid the generously and rather (for modern tastes) over-decorated rooms are some remarkable paintings and original ceilings, including those by **Pietro da Cortona** decorating the reception rooms and the museum's enviable collection of works by **Raphael** and **Titian**.

THE IDIOT IN FLORENCE

Fyodor Mikhailovich Dostoevsky is remembered by a plaque at piazza dei Pitti 22. He sojourned in Florence from 1868–69 and during his stay wrote *The Idiot*.

FLORENTINE ADDRESSES

Many addresses in Forence are followed by the initial 'r', which stands for *rosso*, the Italian for red. In some parts of the city there are two systems of numbering. The red system is used for commercial addresses, and the black for residential.

Right: *Within the extended complex of Palazzo Pitti and the Boboli Garden are five excellent museums.*
Opposite: *The Boboli Garden, built by Cosimo I, is one of Florence's most popular parks.*

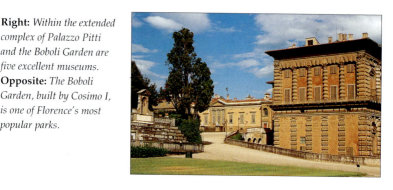

Look out for the intricate *pietra dura* tables made from exquisitely crafted coloured stone, and the stunning crystal chandeliers. Of the paintings, don't miss the magnificent ***Portrait of a Gentleman*** (a fine portrait of Pietro Aretino) and ***The Concert*** by **Titian**; *La Velata* (the Veiled Lady) and the three Madonnas – the round ***Madonna della Seggiola, Madonna dell'Impannata*** and ***Madonna della Granduca*** – all four by **Raphael**; the sublime *Italic Venus* by **Canova**; the uncomfortably realistic *Giuditta* holding Holofernes's head by **Allori**; portrait works by **Rubens**, **Velasquez**, **Tintoretto** and **Van Dyck**; and a late, brooding **Caravaggio**.

The **Apartamenti Reali**, Royal Apartments, which share the same *piano nobile* floor, are also open (same timetable) to the public. They were occupied by the Medici and Lorraine Grand Dukes and then, in the late 1800s, by the Savoy family. They have been restored to reflect this period and show fine furniture.

The **Galleria del Costume** exhibits clothing from the 18th–19th centuries, while the **Museo degli Argenti** holds a large collection of silverware, ceramics and glassware. Both have the same timetable of opening hours as the Galleria Palatina.

Il Giardino di Boboli ★★

One of Florence's favourite places to relax, especially on Sundays, the Boboli Garden (access by way of Palazzo Pitti, open daily except the first and last Monday of each month) brings a wonderful breath of fresh air, cooling fountains and sculptural pleasure to the centre of town.

The Garden was commissioned in 1549 by Cosimo I who wanted to transform the hillside behind the Pitti Palace into a **formal terraced garden**. Plans were made by architect **Tribolo**, who died before it was finished. The garden is divided into two main sections. The lower area is formally laid out on either side of a splendid avenue, the **Viottolone**, which rises in long gentle tiers between areas of evergreens to the circular **Isolotto**. Over 150 statues line the walkways. The 17th-century amphitheatre was conceived and used as a venue for pageants.

Chiesa di Santo Spirito *

This run-down church is located in the large square of the same name, a popular venue for neighbourhood socializing. The church was designed by **Brunelleschi**, though he died long before it was completed. Inside, there are a number of interesting works of art including a fine painting by **Filippino Lippi** (1457–1504), and the impressive late 15th-century sacristy by **Giuliano da Sangallo**.

Cappella Brancacci ***

Not to be missed is this chapel (it is open daily except Wednesday) in **Santa Maria del Carmine**, just a few minutes' walk west of Santo Spirito. The frescoes which adorn the chapel show the hand of three painters: Masolino who began the work, the later artist Filippino Lippi, and the young master, **Masaccio**. His innovative frescoes, executed in 1427, had a profound effect on future generations. Just look at the expression of grief as Adam and Eve are expelled from Paradise; the plasticity of those elegant city figures is particularly impressive when you consider that Masaccio's contemporaries were capable of little more than stiff profiles. These frescoes confirm Masaccio's position as one of the founders of modern painting.

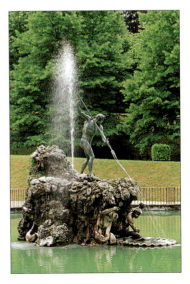

GALLERIA D'ARTE MODERNA

This modern art gallery is also housed in the Pitti Palace (open mornings only, closed 1st, 3rd, 5th Sunday and 2nd and 4th Monday each month) and has Tuscan works from the 18th to the 20th century. Take time to enjoy the paintings produced during the **Macchiaioli Movement**, a school of thought contemporary with the French Impressionists, and for whom nature, realism and the impression of a scene were rendered by *macchia*, marks or daubs of paint. The best exponents were **Nino Costa** (1826–1903), **Giovanni Fattori** (1825–1908), **Silvestro Lega** (1826–95) and **Telemaco Signorini** (1835–1901).

CENTRO STORICO TO NORTH OF DUOMO

Although sightseeing tourists tend to congregate to the south of the Duomo, the web-like streets to the north are the beat of the dedicated art lover for their many *trecento* and *quattrocento* buildings and decorative interiors.

Palazzo Medici-Riccardi ★★★

This imposingly austere palace (via Cavour 3, open daily, except Wednesday; booking advisable) is only open in part to the public. Commissioned by Medici forefather Cosimo the Elder, it was designed by Michelozzo and sold to the Riccardi in the 17th century. Its prime attraction is the **Cappella**, a gem of decoration started in 1459 by **Benozzo Gozzoli**.

This small chapel is entirely painted with frescoes, a colourful patchwork of biblical scenes in which members of Florentine society appear in the guise of illustrative personages – Gozzoli himself is shown wearing a signed hat, Cosimo I sits on a humble but caparisoned mule, while Lorenzo the Magnificent appears as one of the kings in the fresco *Processione dei Magi*.

Cenacolo di Sant'Apollonia ★

Located in the tranquil refectory of the Convent of Sant'Apollonia, at via XXVII Aprile 1 (open mornings, except Monday), is a very fine painting of *The Last Supper* by **Andrea del Castagno** (ca. 1417–57). Painted around 1450, its force is underlined by the rigid architectural elements and strong perspective used by the artist to create the scene, and also by the variety of poses of the apostles and the expressions shown on their faces.

Below: *A popular theme during the Renaissance, this version of* The Last Supper *was painted by Andrea del Castagno for the former convent of Sant'Apollonia.*

PIAZZA SAN MARCO

Via XXVII Aprile and Via Cavour meet at **Piazza San Marco**, site of the Convent and Museum of San Marco, and of the **Accademia**.

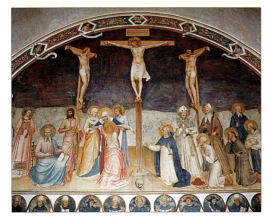

Left: The Crucifixion *by Fra Angelico in San Marco's Chapterhouse.*

Convento e Museo di San Marco **

This Dominican convent (open daily), attached to the Church of San Marco, was built for Cosimo I in 1436 by his favourite architect, Michelozzo (who also designed the library). Its simple plan is a foil for the famous frescoes executed by one of its more celebrated painter-brothers, **Fra Angelico**, who arrived from St Domenico in Fiesole. Fra Angelico went on to become a very successful painter and was canonized in 1983. Antonius was the prior here in the 1450s, while Girolamo Savonarola (*see* panel, page 46) took the office in the late 1490s. Thereafter their paths diverged. Antonius eventually went on to beatification, while Savonarola burned at the stake. Monuments to both are in the church.

Fra Angelico's works are to be found in the Pilgrims' Hospice, where he painted the *Last Judgement* and also the charming *Linaoli Madonna* for the Guild of Linen Merchants. In the Chapterhouse he executed *The Crucifixion* (there is also a *Last Supper* by Ghirlandaio painted for the refectory, now the bookshop). On the first floor, and setting the tone is the very familiar fresco of Fra Angelico's *Annunciation*. Beyond, the monks had their 44 individual cells, all decorated by Fra Angelico and his assistants. The austere quarters used by **Savonarola** contain a few simple possessions used by the prior.

Above: *Michelangelo's world-famous* David.
Opposite: *Gothic Santa Croce dominates the piazza of the same name.*

Galleria dell'Accademia **

It is **Michelangelo's** famous *David* statue which brings most visitors to this Gallery (entrance on via Ricasoli 60, open daily except Monday) but it also houses other important works by this genius, and an art gallery of **Florentine painting** from the 1200s–1800s. Among the sculptural works by Michelangelo are the *Prigioni* or **slaves** (four out of the total six) intended for the tomb of Pope Julius II in Rome and an unfinished *St Matthew*, destined for the Duomo. The sculptor's *David*, familiar but still thrilling, stands in a specially built atrium, a young man about to slay a giant, and an allegory for the powerful Florentine city-state at the turn of the Italian *quattrocento*.

The Galleria dell'Accademia also houses a number of **musical instruments**, decorative arts, and paintings.

PIAZZA DELLA SANTISSIMA ANNUNZIATA

This fine porticoed piazza was designed by architect **Brunelleschi** and its centre is marked by an impressive **Giambologna** equestrian statue of Duke Fernando I.

Santissima Annunziata **

Another conversion by Michelozzo, this church has some well-restored frescoes in its **Chiostrino dei Voti**, dating from the *cinquecento* but executed by some of the biggest names then around – **Andrea del Sarto**, **Jacopo Pontormo** and **Rosso Fiorentino**, among others.

Ospedale degli Innocenti **

On the southeastern side of the piazza, **Brunelleschi** designed this hospital for foundlings and, surprisingly, it still functions as an **orphanage**. Raised by a flight of steps above the square, the 10 slender, grey columns running along its length support a nine-arch colonnade – a beautiful piece of architecture, which the throngs of students seated below, rarely appreciate. Blue and white **roundels** of infants, the work of **Andrea della Robbia**, decorate the space between the arches. Inside, an **art gallery** contains 14th- to 17th-century works by several Florentine painters and sculptors.

Museo Archeologico *

Located at via della Colonna 36, this museum (open mornings, Tuesday to Sunday; also Monday, Tuesday and Thursday afternoons) offers a respite from the myriad works of the Medieval and Renaissance eras. Here you'll step back into Etruscan and Roman times and see such **bronze masterpieces** as the *Chimera* (fourth century BC) and the Etruscan vase, known as the *François Vase*. There are also fine exhibits of **ceramics**, **Egyptian sarcophagi** and **Roman sculpture**.

Opificio delle Pietre Dure *

It's an interesting detour to visit this museum (via degli Alfani 78, open mornings, Monday to Saturday) dedicated to the ancient art of *pietra dura*, (hard stone) slicing **semi-precious** and **coloured stones** into small pieces to create designs on furniture and other decorative arts. This classical art had fallen out of favour until Lorenzo the Magnificent began to commission several works, and subsequently the workshops began to thrive. This museum shows how the stones are cut, various unfinished panels and a reconstruction of a typical *pietra dura* workshop.

PIAZZA DI SANTA CROCE AND AROUND

This large and slightly run-down piazza is a real neighbourhood area of residential Florence and has, as its focal point, the Franciscan basilica of the same name.

MICHELANGELO (1475–1564)

Michelangelo Buonarotti was born in Caprese but grew up in Florence. At 13 years old he was apprenticed to painter Domenico Ghirlandaio, to master painting and fresco techniques before turning his hand to sculpture and the study of anatomy. His first major works in Rome – the **Bacchus** in Florence's Bargello and the **Pietà** in St Peter's – show a gentle sculptor whose figures were yet to gain the power and musculation of his later works. He returned to Florence in 1501 and produced **David** in the Accademia and the lovely **Doni Tondo** in the Uffizi. He then began working on the **Sistine Chapel** in 1508 and finished in 1512; in 1520 he started the sculpture for the **Medici Chapel**. He left for Rome In 1534 and worked as an architect, poet and sculptor until his death there in 1564. The **Casa Buonarroti** (via Ghibellina 70, open mornings except Tuesday) has drawings and memorabilia collected by the great artist and his great-nephew and namesake.

Santa Croce ***

The undeniably Gothic façade of Santa Croce, pointed and multi-coloured, dominates the square. It was possibly conceived by Arnolfo di Cambio in 1294 and completed 150 years later by Vasari who remodelled parts of it in 1560. It was a popular basilica with many of the wealthy Florentine banking families (as witnessed

by their various chapels) and some notable personalities. Alberti, Galileo, Ghiberti, Giotto and Michelangelo are all buried here. There are, in addition, memorials to Dante, playwright Alfieri and Machiavelli.

But it is the **frescoes** in some of the family chapels, the sculptural works and simplicity of the **Pazzi Chapel** which bring most visitors here.

Giotto was commissioned around 1320 to paint frescoes in four chapels but the only surviving works are *Life of St Francis* for the **Bardi Chapel**, *Life of St John the Baptist* and *St John the Evangelist* in the **Peruzzi Chapel**, and the *Coronation of the Virgin* in the **Baroncelli Chapel** (it is believed now that Giotto's workshop was mostly responsible for this painting). This was an enormous undertaking for the artist and it is evident that he had help from his followers in completing the task. Take a moment to look at **Donatello's** *Crucifixion* in the second Bardi Chapel (in the northern transept). It apparently caused upsets in artistic circles when first displayed as it was too realistic.

Work from the church is also housed in the **Museo dell'Opera di Santa Croce**, by the **Cloisters** adjacent to the church. Here the carefully restored *Crucifix* by **Cimabue**, badly damaged in the 1966 flood, now hangs proudly in the refectory. Frescoes by **Taddeo Gaddi** (d. 1366) and his contemporary, **Orcagna**, which were

removed from the church when Vasari remodelled the nave, are on display. An impressive work is **Donatello's** *St Louis of Toulouse*, intended for Orsanmichele (*see* page 34).

Cappella de' Pazzi **

At the far end of the Cloisters stands the Pazzi Chapel, commissioned by the wealthy Pazzi family and designed by **Brunelleschi** who worked on it until 1445. It is probably

one of his most successful works for, in its beautiful simplicity, it has immense harmony. The colour scheme is reduced to grey (travertine) and cream (stucco), the floor plan is a square covered by a dome, with a rectangular apse. **Luca della Robbia** was responsible for the wonderful polychrome terracotta decoration. The **Large Cloisters** were also a late and fine Brunelleschi work. The chapel is open daily.

Piazzale Michelangelo ★★

This is the place (if you haven't climbed the Campanile or the Duomo) to put Florence into **perspective**. On a clear, pollution-free day, the city spreads out beneath as a rusty-coloured carpet of roofs, bisected by the Arno and enclosed by the foothills of the Apennines. It is a popular spot – vendors and tour groups crowd the large square – with a tribute to **Michelangelo** in its centre.

San Miniato al Monte ★★

Behind the piazzale, and accessible up a monumental staircase, is the delightful church of San Miniato. The views of Florence are equally good from here. This small building was erected on the site of an earlier chapel but it was in the 11th century that a **Benedictine monastery** was built on the hillside. Dedicated to the martyr Minias, beheaded by the Romans and possibly buried here, it

Above: *A fine view over the centre of Florence.*
Opposite: *A late work by Brunelleschi, the tranquil cloisters of Santa Croce are a delightful place to unwind.*

CALCIO STORICO

This lively, historic encounter takes place in midsummer. In Renaissance costumes, two teams take to Piazza di Santa Croce which, for the event, becomes a sand-filled arena. Each team of 27 players represents a district, and the object is to get a ball into the opponent's goal. It's a mixture of football, rugby and push-and-shove where feet, heads and fists are all means to the end. Caparisoned horses, noble riders and colourful supporters egg on their teams or deride their adversaries. The game dates back to 1530 when, during Charles V's historic siege, the Florentines played the game with mocking nonchalance.

Above: *The late 15th-century Palazzo Strozzi.*
Opposite: *Fashionable Via de' Tornabuoni.*

served as the order's church. The **harmonious façade**, decorated in geometric green-and-white marble and topped by a gilt mosaic, hides a Romanesque church laid out in basilica form. Among its treasures are the (much-renovated) painted wooden ceiling, the fancy marble floor, and the **Chapel of the Cardinal of Portugal**. The Cardinal's tomb, by **Antonio Rossellino**, is decorated with glazed terracotta, the work of **Luca della Robbia**.

Forte di Belvedere *

This large fortress was commissioned by Ferdinando I in 1590 and built by Buontalenti. Nowadays, it is often used as a venue for large exhibitions. It, too, has a **panoramic view** of the city. Behind it, and leading towards the town centre, is **Via di San Leonardo**, a typical Florentine residential street, which makes a lovely walk down from the Belvedere fortress.

Florentine Palaces **

Back in the heart of the city, a walk through the centre (south of the 19th-century **Piazza della Repubblica**) will take you along original Medieval streets – though most of the period buildings here have been replaced by Renaissance (and later) mansions – and past plenty of imposing palaces, some of which are open to the public.

Almost opposite the main post office, on Via Porta Rossa, lies **Palazzo Davanzati**. The narrow, high façade of this palace contains within its walls the **Museo dell'Antica Casa Fiorentina** (it is currently closed for restoration), a fine representation of Florentine interiors from the 14th–16th centuries. Built originally in the 14th century for a rich merchant, Bernardo Davanzati bought it in the 16th century and added the fashionable loggia level, at the top.

The façade of the **Palazzo di Capitani dei Parte Guelfa** rising above the piazza of the same name is just a couple of right turns away. This 14th-century mansion was the equivalent of party headquarters for the papal-supporting Guelfs. Look out for its exterior staircase.

Borgo Sant'Apostolo runs into **Piazza Santa Trinità**. **Buontalenti** designed the 16th-century façade for the 14th-century church, but look how well the earlier, 11th-century structure has been incorporated.

Via de' Tornabuoni **

Smart Via de' Tornabuoni, which runs from Santa Trinità to Via de' Panzani, has been in fashion ever since the Tornabuoni constructed their 14th-century palazzo here. Some near neighbours include the **Spini-Feroni**, whose 13th-century mansion still survives at No. 2, and the **Strozzis**, situated at the corner of Via degli Strozzi and Via de' Tornabuoni. **Palazzo Strozzi**, with one of the most harmonious Renaissance façades, was built for Filippo Strozzi by a series of architects culminating in **Simone del Pollaiuolo**.

At the north end of Via de' Tornabuoni, the Antinoris built their home, **Palazzo Antinori**, giving the piazza the same name. This marvellous, (relatively) small palace was designed by **Giuliano da Maiano** in the mid-*quattrocento*.

The deconsecrated church, San Pancrazio, now houses the **Museo Marino Marini** (*see* panel, page 52).

Palazzo Rucellai, on the fashionable **Via della Vigna Nuova**, benefits from an intricate and very beautiful façade incorporating the three architectural orders, and plenty of windows. It was built during the 1440s for

MUSEO MARINO MARINI

This museum (Piazza San Pancrazio, open daily, except Tuesday) has a fine exhibition of sculpture by this talented painter turned sculptor. Born in 1901, he trained in Florence but worked mainly in Milan. During the 1930s, the artist's interest in Etruscan and Classical Greek art influenced some of his most familiar works, especially those of man and horse, which he executed in both wood and bronze.

Giovanni Rucellai by **Bernardo Rossellino**, from designs drawn up by Alberti. Today, the new neighbours are also in the fashion business: Gucci, Armani and Valentino.

It is just a couple of minutes' walk to the huge 16th–17th-century **Palazzo Corsini**, a Baroque palace which dominates the Lungarno Corsini.

Ognissanti *

All Saints' church, or Ognissanti, is located about halfway down Borgo Ognissanti. The original 13th-century church was rebuilt during the 17th century. Botticelli is buried here, but it is the important frescoes in the church which attract most visitors.

The *Cenacolo* by **Domenico Ghirlandaio** (1449–94) is a beautiful 1480 rendition of the *Last Supper*, painted in the church's refectory. Although he was not a highly innovative artist, Ghirlandaio was a popular one and in this masterfully lit rendition he uses perspective devices, and very naturalistic poses to create the illusion of the Supper in an alcove. He also painted the *St Jerome* and the *Madonna della Misericordia* in the main church.

Santa Maria Novella **

The gloriously ornate green-and-white marble façade of this Dominican church dominates the square of the same name. Humanist and architect **Alberti** complemented **Jacopo Talenti's** Gothic lower half of the façade with a fine Renaissance upper section. It is one of Florence's most important buildings. The existing church complex, complete with cloisters, was constructed in the 14th and 15th centuries and was funded by the wealthy Rucellai family. Inside, there are finely decorated chapels built by a number of prominent Florentine

Left: *Tourists discover an excellent selection of Tuscan leather and handicrafts in the market around San Lorenzo.*

Opposite: *The Dominican church of Santa Maria Novella is one of the city's most important and houses a wealth of fine art.*

families: the Bardi, Strozzi and Rucellai. Among the artistic treasures, **Masaccio** painted a fine *Trinità*; **Domenico Ghirlandaio** painted a magnificent and extensive fresco cycle of the *Life of the Virgin* and *Life of St John the Baptist*, probably his finest work; **Paolo Uccello** painted some excellent frescoes in the **Chiostro Verde**; and in the Cappellone degli Spagnoli are mid-*quattrocento* frescoes by **Andrea Firenza**.

SAN LORENZO

The area around the church of San Lorenzo held particular importance to the Medici family: it was their parish, their local church, and Cosimo commissioned his family residence there in 1444. Over 500 years later, the district of San Lorenzo still bears the mark of this dynasty.

San Lorenzo **

The church that we see today (behind the grey exterior still awaiting its marble finish) was remodelled by **Brunelleschi** from 1420 onward, and stands on the site of a previous paleo-Christian chapel. It is one of the most important churches in the city and its restrained

---

FASHION IN FLORENCE

An eye for contemporary clothes? A figure for fashion? A well-stacked wallet? Then a little retail therapy awaits you in central Florence. Via de' Tornabuoni is the place to source the most exclusive designs. **Gucci** (who also pops up in Via Vigna Nuova), **Prada**, **Trussardi**, **Max Mara**, **Yves Saint Laurent**, and **Gianni Versace** will clothe you; **Cartier**, **Damiani**, **Bulgari** and **Tiffany** offer a selection of fine jewels and priceless baubles; **Genny**, **Bottega Veneta**, **Hermès**, **Salvatore Ferragamo** and **Louis Vuitton** will take care of the bags, shoes and luggage. After which, if you still have energy, Via della Vigna Nuova can provide the goods with **Valentino**, **Mila Schön**, **Giorgio Armani** or **Etro**.

Right: *The dark grey stone chosen by architect Michelangelo gives a note of grandeur to the unusual stairs at the entrance of the Laurenziana Library.*

LAPI@FLORENCE.NET.IT?

An Italian academic has recently uncovered evidence which shows that the ubiquitous symbol of the internet era was used by Florentine merchants over 500 years ago. The @ sign represents an amphora, the terracotta jar in which liquid and grains were transported in the ancient world, and has been found in a letter written by Francesco Lapi, a merchant describing the cargo of ships due to arrive in Spain from the New World. The academic race is on to see who has the oldest documentary evidence: Venice was the last to discontinue use of the amphora measure, but Florence was the foremost medieval banking centre.

elegance is the hallmark of earlier Medici commissions. Brunelleschi designed the church with a nave and two aisles but included new details that were to characterize Renaissance art: curved arches, Corinthian columns, pilasters, unadorned surfaces and decorative cornices. Head for the **Sacrestia Vecchia**, the Old Sacristy, also designed by Brunelleschi, decorated by Donatello and recently carefully renovated, admiring Donatello's marvellous bronze doors as you enter, and the calm atmosphere created by the use of the grey *pietra serena* and light coloured walls. **Taddeo Gaddi** painted the triptych *Madonna and Child* and, back in the church, there is an attractive *Annunciation* by **Filippo Lippi**. Before leaving the church, in which Donatello is buried, it is worth looking at the butter-coloured cloisters, accessible off the northern aisle.

Biblioteca Medicea Laurenziana *

The Laurenziana Library (open mornings, except Sunday) was originally commissioned by Cosimo the Elder and extended under his grandson, Lorenzo the Magnificent.

It contains a priceless collection of approximately 10,000 works, including original Greek and Roman manuscripts, a work by **Virgil** with margin annotations by Petrarch, works by **Petrarch**, **Machiavelli**, and Lorenzo the Magnificent's *Book of Hours*. Of note architecturally is the *vestibolo* (vestibule) which was decorated by **Michelangelo** and includes a magnificent flight of curved stairs in solemn grey designed by Michelangelo, but executed by **Ammannati** after the architect had left for Rome. The **Sala di Lettura**, the Reading Room, is likewise impressive, the wooden coffered ceiling and wooden desks both by Michelangelo.

Cappelle Medicee ***

The Medici Chapels (situated at Piazza Madonna degli Aldobrandini, open daily except Monday) were Michelangelo's first architectural commission. You enter via the later Cappella dei Principi, the dark marble mausoleum of the Grand Dukes, and continue on to the **Sagrestia Nuova**. Michelangelo began work on the New Sacristy in 1521, after having worked on the façade of San Lorenzo. He had toiled in the quarries for five years, labouring over the architectural details, but the Medici cancelled his contract for the façade, replacing it with the more pressing need for a suitable family chapel and mausoleum. This chapel, intended as the last resting place for Medici family members, includes the tombs of both **Lorenzo the Magnificent** and his brother **Giuliano**. It is solemn and yet beautiful – thanks largely to Michelangelo's superb, imaginative sculptures lounging across the monumental tombs.

> **MERCATO DI SAN LORENZO**
>
> This is Florence's most popular market, a potpourri of outside stalls swamping the streets around the piazza, and a large covered produce market. The locals shop early in the morning, selecting the best fish, vegetables and fruit, while the tourists stroll along later, and compare prices and merchandise at the many leather stalls. Belts, bags, wallets and clothing (including inexpensive cashmere) can all be bargains for those who care to haggle with good humour.

Below: *Michelangelo's powerful sculptures of* Night *and* Day *for Giuliano's tomb in the Cappelle Medicee.*

Florence at a Glance

BEST TIMES TO VISIT

Florence in **winter** can be rainy, but the museums are crowd-free and there are rarely queues. The gardens and countryside are more attractive during **autumn** and **spring**, though the crowds are already there. The **summer** season (Easter to mid-October) is crowded and sometimes hot. Rainy days are few.

GETTING THERE

The **international airport** at **Florence** (Amerigo Vespucci, tel: 055 30615) has frequent **taxi** services from the airport to the centre. Airlines serving this airport include Meridiana, Sabena, Lufthansa and Air France. **Pisa** has a much bigger **international airport** (Galileo Galilei, tel: 050 500707). A **train** service from the airport passes by the city on its one-hour trip to Florence. Airlines serving this airport include British Airways, Ryanair, Alitalia, Lufthansa, Air France and Sabena. By **road**, Florence is on the toll-paying **Autostrada del Sole**, the A1, which links Milan with Rome. It also has good roads to all the other towns in Tuscany. For **drivers**, parking is a problem as cars are not permitted in the city centre. Public **car parks** include Fortezza da Basso and the underground car park, Piazza Stazione. Eurolines run 3 weekly direct **bus** services between London (Victoria) and Florence. Travel

time is just under 16 hours. Information from Eurolines (National Express) in the UK, enquiries, tel: 09 9080 8080. Florence is on the Milan–Rome **railway** line, with frequent services, stopping at Florence between these two cities.

GETTING AROUND

Once in Florence, the best is to **walk**; the pedestrian-only *centro storico* is compact. White **taxis** (*see* below) are also available. Four electric-powered town **buses** ply the streets. The **railway** station is the terminus for two lines. Tickets for single journeys, valid for one hour each, must be bought in advance from *tabacchi*, kiosks selling newspapers, shops displaying the ATAF sticker, or the station. **Bike** enthusiasts can rent from **Florence by Bike**, via San Zanobia 120r/122r, tel: 055 488992. **Taxis** are available by contacting tel: 055 4242, 055 4390 and 055 4798.

WHERE TO STAY

Florence is very expensive and the budget traveller may have to pay a premium, or opt for accommodation outside town.

LUXURY

Plaza Hotel Lucchesi, lungarno della Zecca Vecchia 38, tel: 055 26236, fax: 055 2480921, website: www.plazalucchesi.it South-facing, just minutes from Ponte Vecchio. Best rooms overlook the Arno.

Gallery Hotel Art, vicolo dell'Oro 5, tel: 055 27263, fax: 055 268557, website: lungarnohotels.it Renovated, modern, zen hotel. Near Ponte Vecchio yet quiet.

Hotel Londra, via Jacopo da Diacceto 16/20, tel: 055 27390, fax: 055 210682, website: www.hotellondra.com Quiet, comfortable, near station and Santa Maria Novella.

Savoy, piazza della Repubblica 7, tel: 055 27351, fax: 055 2735888, website: www.rfhotels.com A new look for the Savoy, renovated in sumptuous style.

Hotel Mirage, via Baracca 231/18, tel: 055 352011, fax: 055 374096, website: www.hotelmirage.it In suburbs, comfortable hotel with parking. Buses to centre.

Hotel J and J, via di Mezzo 20, tel: 055 263121, fax: 055 240 282, website: jandjhotel.com A 10-minute walk from the centre, in former convent. Tastefully furnished rooms.

MID-RANGE

Pensione Annalena, via Romana 34, tel: 055 222402 or 055 229600, fax: 055 222403, website: www.hotelannalena.it In old palace, once belonging to Lorenzo the Magnificent's grandfather. Now a good, traditional pension, a favourite with returning guests.

Hotel Porta Rossa, via Porta Rossa 19, tel: 055 287551, fax: 282179. Old-style hotel, large rooms, in centre of town.

Florence at a Glance

Fiorentina, via dei Fossi 12, tel: 055 219530, fax: 055 287105. Spacious rooms, a short walk from station, River Arno or Via de' Tornabuoni.

Scoti, via de' Tornabuoni 7, tel/fax: 055 292128. Small hotel. Pedestrian-only zone.

Toscana, via del Sole 8, tel/fax: 055 213156. Small, comfortable and very central, near Santa Maria Novella.

WHERE TO EAT

LUXURY

Enoteca Pinchiorri, via Ghibellina 87, tel: 055 242777. Courtyard dining. Arguably Florence's best address.

Osteria del Caffè Italiano, via Isola delle Stinche 11/13r, tel: 055 289368. Excellent Tuscan fare, limited menu. Reservations recommended.

Taverna del Bronzino, via delle Ruote 25/27r, tel: 055 495220. Near Piazza Independenza. Good value, fine wines.

Enoteca Pane e Vino, via di San Niccolò 70, tel: 055 247 6956. Near Ponte alle Grazie. Set menu or à la carte, wines.

MID-RANGE

La Cantinetta Antinori, piazza Antinori 3, tel: 055 292234. Antinori wines (excellent) in smart *enoteca* ambience. Good Tuscan food.

Buca Lapi, via del Trebbio 1, tel: 055 213768. Authentic *trattoria* (one of the oldest in the city) popular with locals. Range of Tuscan specialities.

Il Latini, via del Palchetti 6, tel: 055 210916. Oozing ambience, just off fashionable Via della Vigna Nuova. Semi-set menu. Booking essential.

Il Paiolo, via del Corso 42r, tel: 055 2150191. Tuscan cuisine in this popular central restaurant. Closed Sundays.

Trattoria La Carabaccia, via Palazzuolo 190r, tel: 055 214 782. Family-run. Near Santa Maria Novella.

La Maremma, via Verdi 16r, tel: 055 244615. Near Santa Croce, a traditional Florentine restaurant, good ambience.

BUDGET

Trattoria del Carmine, piazza del Carmine 18r, tel: 055 218601. Inside-outside dining in reasonably priced restaurant. Wide choice of Tuscan food.

Osteria Santo Spirito, piazza Santo Spirito 16r, tel: 055 2382383. Good, wholesome Italian food. Outdoor seating.

Da Ruggero, via Senese 89r (Porta Romana), tel: 055 220 542. Home cooking, popular trattoria. Bookings advisable.

Le Mossacce, via del Proconsolo 55r, tel: 055 294361. Popular Tuscan fare. Central.

TOURS AND EXCURSIONS

CAF Viaggi, via Roma 4, tel: 055 283200, fax: 055 2382790.

Amici del Turismo, via Cavour 36, tel: 055 218413, fax: 055 283892.

USEFUL CONTACTS

APT, the Tourist Promotion Office for Florence, is situated at via Manzoni 16, Florence, tel: 055 23320, fax: 055 2346286. Not very central. **APT** also has premises at via Cavour 1r, tel: 055 290832, Piazza Stazione (Railway Station), tel: 055 212245, and Borgo Santo Croce 29r, tel: 055 2340444.

Post Office (Ufficio Postale), via Pellicceria 3, tel: 055 27741.

Alitalia, vicolo dell'Oro 1, Florence, tel: 055 27881.

Car Hire: Europcar, borgo Ognissanti 53r, tel: 055 2360072; Hertz, via Maso Finiguerra 33/r, tel: 055 2398205; Maxirent, borgo Ognissanti 155r, tel: 055 2654207.

British Consulate: Lungarno Corsini 2, tel: 055 284133.

US Consulate: Lungarno Vespucci 38, tel: 055 2398276.

FLORENCE	J	F	M	A	M	J	J	A	S	O	N	D
AVERAGE TEMP. °C	10	12	15	19	22	24	28	25	24	20	15	10
AVERAGE TEMP. °F	50	53	59	66	72	75	82	77	75	68	59	50
HOURS OF SUN DAILY	4	5	6	6	7	9	9	9	7	6	4	3
RAINFALL mm	62	60	68	69	72	56	23	48	84	100	104	77
RAINFALL in	2.4	2.3	2.6	2.7	2.8	2.1	0.9	1.8	3.3	3.9	4.0	3.0
DAYS OF RAINFALL	8	8	8	8	7	4	3	3	5	9	10	11

3
Around Florence

The River Arno cuts a fertile swathe through the hills around Florence, providing good agricultural land amidst the hilly topography. From initial farming settlements, the Arno's rural villages prospered into small towns which, by the second millennium, increasingly fell under the domination of up-and-coming Florence.

From the Tuscan capital, these towns are just a short journey away by car, bus or train. Though they can easily be explored in a day, they also have excellent and affordable accommodation, and thus provide an interesting and more relaxing alternative to staying in the centre of Florence.

Fiesole rises above Florence and presents the visitor, weather permitting, with a fine panorama of the city. It also boasts a rich past and some interesting monuments. **Prato** and **Pistoia**, both formerly individual small towns, are now not only part of the urban development around Florence but also provincial capitals. Pistoia has a marvellous *centro storico*. The Medici built villas on the outskirts, and some of these can be seen in the **Mugello** area.

To the west, **Montecatini Terme** has been curing Tuscan aches and ailments for centuries. The nearby town of **Collodi**, known for its magnificent Villa Garzoni, and tiny village of **Vinci**, birthplace of the great Leonardo, are both worth visiting.

South of Florence, a series of interesting monasteries and churches claim attention – the **Certosa del Galluzzo**, **Certaldo** and **Impruneta** – before the road extends into the Chianti Hills and the rolling panorama of vine-clad hills.

DON'T MISS

*** **Fiesole:** hilltop town with great views.
*** **Chianti region:** for wine tasting and discovering small Tuscan towns.
** **Villa Garzoni:** a fine Italian garden at Collodi.
** **Pistoia:** see the Medieval Piazza del Duomo and its surrounding buildings.
** **Certosa del Galluzzo:** a lavish charterhouse with fine frescoes by Pontormo.
* **Prato:** visit the Duomo for the Filippo Lippi frescoes.

Opposite: *The elaborate gardens of Villa Garzoni in Collodi.*

Around Florence

NORTH OF FLORENCE

Although one tends to drive quickly into industrial areas and unappealing suburbs, there are a couple of important places to visit north of the city.

Fiesole ***

From Florence it is only about 8km (5 miles) to Fiesole and the attractive small hilltop town was much appreciated by 19th-century travellers; *A Room with a View* was set here. The views and the area's delightful rural roads are what bring most visitors to the town and from the **Piazza Mino da Fiesole**, a tribute to the local sculptor, Florence fans out below. This is the town centre, a touristy area in which cafés and vendors capitalize on foreign trade. The nearby **Duomo** hosts two tombs by Mino da Fiesole.

It would also be a shame to miss the massive Etruscan walls, or the Roman Theatre in the **Zona Archeologica** (open daily, except first Monday of month). The **Museo Archeologico** (open as above) displays some exceptional Etruscan statues and other finds from the Zona.

San Domenico di Fiesole (located between Fiesole and Florence) is the church where Fra Angelico took his vows; see his 1430 painting of the *Virgin, Saints and Angels*.

IL MUGELLO

The bucolic valley of the River Sieve, due north of Florence, has long been a favourite place for secondary residences. The Medici family originated here.

Borgo San Lorenzo *

Borgo San Lorenzo, a small provincial town groaning with industrialization, is the main urban centre of the area. It has buildings dating from the 12th century and

Opposite: Prato's unusual external pulpit, designed by Michelozzo, originally held panels by Donatello (these are now in the Museo dell'Opera del Duomo).

CASHMERE SAVINGS

Direct sales from the factory enable visitors in the Prato area to make excellent savings on cashmere products. Made of Mongolian cashmere, woven in Prato for distribution throughout the country, Maglieria Artigiana, via del Mandorlo 19/21, is worth a visit. For information and directions, tel: 0574 550384 or fax: 0574 571943.

although it was severely affected in the 1919 earthquake and 1944 bombing, it is still worth seeing the faithfully reconstructed **Palazzo Pretorio** in the Piazza Garibaldi and the church of **San Lorenzo**, a 12th–13th-century building.

Cafaggiolo *

Approximately 10km (nearly 7 miles) away lies the Villa at Cafaggiolo (not usually open to the public), Cosimo the Elder's first residence. Michelozzo was charged with converting an earlier fortress into the Medici summer home, and the forbidding building can be glimpsed without difficulty from the roadside.

Prato *

A veritable Medieval oasis in the midst of a rather ugly industrial landscape, old Prato is fascinating and quite easily accessible from Florence. For centuries it has been renowned for its wool cloth, and the town's rich merchants erected fine buildings.

The first stop should be the **Duomo**, resplendent with **Filippo Lippi's** fresco cycle of the *Life of St John* and the *Life of St Stephen*, and an elegant synthesis of early Romanesque and later Gothic styles. The **Chapel of the Holy Girdle** houses the Virgin's famous girdle relic; it is brought out into public five times a year. On leaving, look up at Michelozzo's unusual external pulpit; a stunning piece of work. **Donatello's** original panels are now in the **Museo dell'Opera del Duomo** (open mornings Wednesday to Monday; afternoons Monday, and Wednesday to Saturday). Just a couple of minutes away, in Piazza del Comune, is the rather forbidding 13th-century **Palazzo Pretorio**. Another structure worth seeing, from the same era, is the **Castello dell'Imperatore**, situated next to the Renaissance **Santa Maria delle Carceri**.

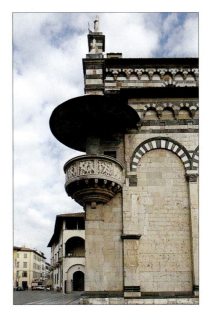

MONTECATINI TERME

The Romans loved their spas, and their descendants are no exception. Montecatini Terme is one of the country's prime spots for taking the waters, relaxing, shopping in its elegant streets or treating a number of ailments including digestive disorders, skin complaints, rheumatism and arthritis. Mud and spa baths, massage and constant consumption of mineralized water are complemented by other, alternative and avant-garde therapies. The Terme buildings were laid out in elegant style just over a century ago.

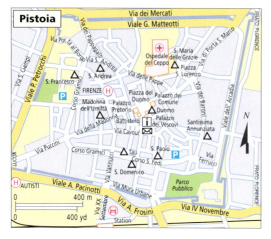

TOWARDS THE NORTHWEST

Heading west, there are plenty of easily accessible places to visit in the provinces of Pistoia, Prato and Lucca.

Pistoia **

Beyond the industry and ornamental plant cultivation around Pistoia there exists a Medieval heart. It lies 36km (nearly 23 miles) either by motorway or the *strada statale* from Florence and like the larger city, has a fascinating past. Heart of Pistoia is its **Piazza del Duomo**, a Medieval centre lined by period buildings including the **Duomo**, **Palazzo Pretorio**, **Palazzo del Comune** and **Palazzo dei Vescovi**. It is here that the Medieval **Bear Joust** takes place every year, complete with historic costumes and a (fake) bear. Were it not for the occasional phone line and motorcycle, you'd believe you were in a time warp.

The delicate arcades and later porches of the **Duomo**, and striped marble decoration above them, remind one of Pisa's cathedral. Part of the interior was remodelled in

Below: *Pistoia has retained its distinctive Medieval centre. Pictured here are the Duomo and its Campanile.*

Baroque style but the highlight of the cathedral remains **l'altare di San Jacopo**, the altarpiece of St James. Its Medieval gold and silver-work positively gleams as the light gives form to the hundreds (literally) of figures illustrating both Old and New Testaments. The work was commissioned in 1287 and not completed until the mid-15th century.

The **Battistero**, an octagonal baptistry decorated on the outside with green and white marble (but rather bare on the inside), dates from the 14th century, and is believed to have been designed by the Tuscan sculptor, **Andrea Pisano**. Statues on the tympanum are thought to have been sculpted

by Andrea's two sons, Nino and Tommaso. Towering over the Duomo is the multi-styled **Campanile**, with its unusually plain bottom half in direct contrast to the arcaded top levels.

Next to the Duomo is the Bishops' Palace, **Palazzo dei Vescovi**, (open for guided tours, Tuesday, Thursday and Friday) now housing archaeological exhibits including vases, Etruscan funerary urns and Roman ceramics. It also holds the Duomo's treasures including reliquaries, ecclesiastical clothing and statues.

The **Ospedale del Ceppo**, 200m (220yd) to the north of the Duomo, is noted for Giovanni della Robbia's delightful terracotta frieze, glazed in harmonizing colours and for the complementary roundels. Founded originally in 1277, it still functions as a hospital.

Villa at Poggio a Caiano **

Just 17km (10 miles) outside Florence, and some 8km (5 miles) from Prato is the Medici villa at Poggio a Caiano (open daily, except the second and third Monday each month). This country house was bought by Lorenzo the Magnificent, who commissioned architect **Giuliano da Sangallo** in 1480 to modify it for his own needs. It was sumptuously revamped (the up-and-coming Mannerist painter, **Pontormo**, was responsible for the 1521 frescoes) and received many notables during the Medici tenure, followed by sundry European nobles and the kings of Italy. Recent interior renovations have returned it to its 19th-century style. Approximately 5km (3 miles) away, the huge hilltop Medici villa at **Artimino** is sometimes open for visits.

Above: *In use for more than 700 years, the Ospedale del Ceppo still functions as a hospital.*

THE MAIN MEDICI

From humble merchants to Grand Dukes to Queens, the Medici influenced history and the fortunes of more than just Florence.
Cosimo il Vecchio, Cosimo the Elder, 1389–1464.
Pietro il Gottoso, Piero the Gouty, 1414–69.
Lorenzo il Magnifico, Lorenzo the Magnificent, 1449–92.
Giovanni de Medici, Pope Leo X, 1475–1521.
Lorenzo II, Duke of Urbino, 1492–1519.
Francesco I, Grand Duke, 1541–87.
Catherine de Medici, married King Henri II, Queen of France, 1519–89.
Maria de Medici, widow of Henri IV, mother of Louis XIII, 1573–1642.

Above: *Pinocchio puppets for sale in a Florence store.*
Opposite: *A roundel by Luca della Robbia decorates the Certosa del Galluzzo.*

Collodi *

Collodi is home to one of Italy's most endearing fictional characters – **Pinocchio**, the wooden string puppet whose nose grew longer when he lied. Die-hard Pinocchio fans should take their children to the **Parco di Pinocchio** where, within a pine wood, various Pinocchio characters grace a marked walk.

Collodi is also the site of a much-visited formal Italian garden, still in its original state, attached to the mid-17th-century **Villa Garzoni**. This is Italian Baroque gardening at its best: different levels and terraces combine architecture with the flora. Low hedges, symmetrical plants (not to mention flights of steps and copies of Hellenistic statues) and bright flowers are laid out to present an orderly and balanced garden. Topiary figures, lily ponds, grottoes, a *scala d'acqua* (water staircase), statues that spout unexpected jets, and a small theatre give the garden its delightful character.

WEST OF FLORENCE

The small village of **Vinci**, in beautiful hilly countryside, might never have been visited by tourists if it were not for its most famous son, **Leonardo**. He was born in Anchiano, a couple of kilometres north of Vinci. His presumed birthplace, the **Casa di Leonardo**, is open (daily) to tourists and offers you a few original architectural features but the most interesting stop is a the **Museo Leonardiano** (same timetable) where various models have been fashioned after his engineering designs.

San Miniato *

The pleasant hilltop town of San Miniato, some 37km (23 miles) from Florence, knew considerable prosperity in the past. It was the Tuscan residence of the **Holy Roman Emperors** and later, during the Renaissance, home to many noble families.

Writer **Carlo Lorenzini**, better known as Carlo Collodi, author of *Pinocchio*, is buried in San Miniato cemetery while, still very much alive, cinema's two talented **Taviani brothers**, Paolo and Vittorio, were born in the town. The **Museo Diocesano d'Arte Sacra** (open mornings and afternoons, except Monday, from Easter to December; otherwise weekends and public holidays only) and the **Spiazza del Castello** are both worth visiting, the former for its good collection of sculpture and paintings, the latter for its **panoramic views** of the Arno valley and the Apennines. Don't miss, either, the delicate mural designs above the **Medieval shops** in Piazza della Repubblica.

SOUTH OF FLORENCE

The road to Siena, much travelled during the Middle Ages and Renaissance, also offers the modern traveller many interesting sights.

Certosa del Galluzzo **

Some 6.5km (4 miles) from Florence, the great Carthusian monastery, the Charterhouse at **Galluzzo** (open mornings and afternoons, except Monday), was commissioned by **Niccolò Acciaiuoli**, a Florentine banking magnate of the 14th century. His family are buried in the church. Its **cloisters**, with a portico of columns decorated with **della Robbia roundels**, is where the monks had their cells. One of these is open to the public. The **Palazzo Acciaiuoli** houses the *pinacoteca* (art gallery), the highlight of which are 16th-century frescoes by the religious Mannerist painter, Pontormo.

LEONARDO DA VINCI

Leonardo, one of the creators of the High Renaissance, was born in 1452. He trained as a painter under Verocchio and by the late 1470s had a fine reputation. His first existing masterpiece, the unfinished *Adoration of the Magi* (1481, Uffizi) shows his talents for observation. He went to Milan in 1483 and painted the *Last Supper* in 1497. In 1500 he studied anatomy in Florence, started *Madonna and Child with St Anne* and completed the *Mona Lisa*. Appointed Engineer and Painter to Louis XII in 1507, he moved to France where he died in 1519.

Below: *Many country homes function as hotels.*

Certaldo

Giovanni Boccaccio (1312–75) is this town's most celebrated personality. It is not certain whether he was born in the Medieval heart of town, but he certainly died here and is commemorated by a statue. On the way to Certaldo Alto (old Certaldo) you'll find the **Casa del Boccaccio** where he lived later in life – a museum cum library with editions and translations of his works. Boccaccio is buried in the church, Santi Michele e Jacopo.

Impruneta

A small town historically known for its bricks, pots and tiles, Impruneta still deals in terracotta. Stop and look at the pottery in the **Basilica di Santa Maria dell'Impruneta**, in the centre of town. Although the Basilica suffered war damage, it was subsequently well restored. Michelozzo is credited with two of the chapels and there are some pretty **della Robbia** works. To the south of Impruneta, at Ferrone, the road joins the Via Chiantigiana, which runs through the famous Chianti wine-growing district.

The small hilltop town of **Barberino Val d'Elsa**, some 34km (21 miles) from Florence, sprawls beyond its walls into rather less picturesque modern architecture. The renovated old town is accessible via the town gate, **Porta Senese**, piercing its strong Medieval walls. **Piazza Barberini** marks the centre, and of note here are the Renaissance **Palazzo Pretorio** and also the library housed in the Medieval **Ospedale dei Pellegrini**.

Taking the side road through the pretty *Colli Fiorentini* (the Florentine hills), from Barberino Val d'Elsa through Linari to Poggibonsi, it is worth stopping at the small church of **Sant'Appiano**, 6km (nearly 4 miles) away. This early Christian church was originally built in the 10th century but was rebuilt in the 12th century when its campanile fell in on the nave. Take a look, too, at the small cloisters, and the **Antiquarium** (open Saturday and Sunday afternoons only) which displays Etruscan and Roman finds from the neighbourhood.

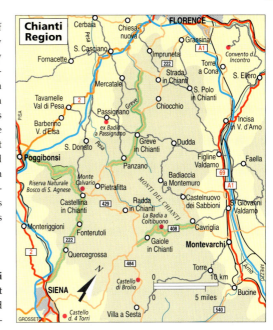

THE CHIANTI REGION

The sloping hills of **Monti del Chianti**, peaking at 893m (nearly 3000ft) and extending through the border between the provinces of Florence and Siena, are picture postcard-perfect Tuscany: handsome woods, cleared in part for neat rows of vines, the grey haze of olive groves punctuated by the sharp forms of cypress trees, attractive old *case caloniche* (farmhouses), small churches, historic abbeys and Medieval hilltop villages, crowned by their castles.

Far from being raw nature, it is a landscape tamed by man, fashioned for his needs and now one in which its traditional agriculture – wine production, olive oil and fruits – rubs shoulders with the influx of new landlords: foreigners seeking to immerse themselves into the tranquillity and beauty of this bucolic landscape.

Greve in Chianti **

At the heart of the Florentine Chianti region, Greve in Chianti takes its name from the river which flows through it. It is a leading centre for Chianti and also a regional market town. The unusual triangular 'square',

Piazza Matteotti, forms the heart of town. It is lined
with two long arcades, narrowing to the side occupied
by the small church of **Santa Croce**, rebuilt in neo-
Classical style on the site of a former church.

On the hills either side of Greve are small country
roads leading to some attractive villages and individual
(often carefully renovated) castles which, for those who
like wandering through the countryside, are worthwhile
exploring. Among these is Medieval **Montefioralle**, on
the road towards Tavarnelle Val di Pesa. Continuing
onward up and over the hill for another 6–7km (some
4 miles), you'll come to the Badia a Passignano.

Badia a Passignano *

The ex-Abbey at Passignano has a superb position on
a small hill that affords a peaceful panorama over vineyards and cypresses. Badia a Passignano was founded
in the late 11th century and the village has grown in
its shadow. The church, dedicated to the Archangel
St Michael, is decorated with frescoes by a 16th-century
local artist, **Domenico Cresti**. In the spacious refectory
of the monastery there is a large *Last Supper* by the
Ghirlandaio brothers.

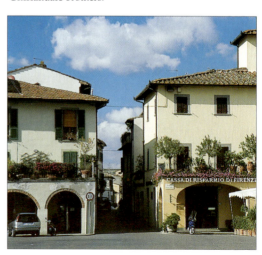

Right: *Triangular Piazza
Matteotti, in Greve in
Chianti, is the social heart of
this wine-producing town.*

Around Florence at a Glance

The countryside is lovely in **spring** and **autumn**. **Summer** can be hot and crowded. **Winter** can be bleak, but it can also be crisp and sunny, especially after Christmas.

Most people use the **airports** at Florence (Amerigo Vespucci, tel: 055 30615), 4km (2.5 miles) northwest of town, or Pisa (Galileo Galilei, tel: 050 500707) just 3km (under 2 miles) south of Pisa and 75km (48 miles) from Florence. A **train** service from the airport passes by the city on its one-hour trip to Florence. There is an excellent network of **roads** radiating out from Florence. From Florence's Railway Station there are **buses** to many destinations. The No. 7 goes to Fiesole; No. 11 to Settignano; No. 13 to Piazza Michelangelo. Lazzi have frequent bus services from Florence. Prato is on the main Milan–Rome **railway** line. Another line runs from Florence to Viareggio, via Pistoia, Montecatini and Lucca.

The easiest way is by private or hired **car**. There are also **bus** services between the main towns, and **rail** services (*see* above). Prato is 17km (10 miles) from Florence, Pistoia 36km (22 miles), San Miniato 37km (23 miles) and Greve in Chianti 31km (20 miles).

LUXURY

Villa San Michele, via Doccia 4, Fiesole, tel: 055 5678200, fax: 055 5678250. A magnificent place with fine gardens.
Villa Vannini, villa di Piteccio, Pistoia, tel: 0573 42031, fax: 0573 26331. Small villa 6km (4 miles) north of Pistoia (car needed). Attractive rural setting.
Villa di Vignamaggio, Greve in Chianti, tel: 055 8544840, fax: 055 8544468. Mini apartments in luxury villa (used in Branagh's *Much Ado About Nothing*). Impressive scenery.

MID-RANGE

Villa Campestri, Vicchio del Mugello, direction Campestri, tel: 055 8490107, fax: 055 8490108. Very comfortable rural villa in fine park ambience.
Osteria del Vacario, via Rivellino 3, Certaldo Alto, tel/fax: 055 668228. In old part of Certaldo, a small hotel with good restaurant.
Villa Rucellai, via di Canneto 16, Prato, tel: 0574 460392. Amid industrialized Prato, a pool of calm and good taste.
Relais Fattoria Valle Panzano, via Case Sparse 56, km28, SS222, Greve in Chianti, tel: 055 852482, fax: 055 852716. Restored 19th-century villa with panoramic views.

BUDGET

Alexandra, via dei Martiri 82, Vinci, tel: 0571 56224, fax: 0571 567972. Mid-sized hotel with a good restaurant.

Villa Sorriso, via Gramsci 21, Fiesole, tel: 055 59027, fax: 055 59978075. Comfortable small hotel off central piazza.

LUXURY

Il Piraña, via Valentini 110, Prato, tel: 0574 25746. Excellent restaurant with fine fish and seafood specialities.
La Panacea del Bartonlini, via dei Bosconi 58/A, Fiesole, tel: 055 548932. Great views and fine Tuscan food with some inventive dishes.

MID-RANGE

Osteria del Vacario, Certaldo, *see* Where to Stay.
Il Feriolo, via Faentina 32, on Rt 32, 15km (10 miles) south of Borgo San Lorenzo, tel: 055 8409928. Medieval building; good restaurant. Tuscan fare.

BUDGET

Antica Fiaschetteria, piazza Lippi 4, Prato, tel: 0574 41225. Popular with locals, inexpensive snacks, Tuscan specialities.
Il Ritrovo d' Iccio, via dei Fabbri 7, Pistoia, tel: 0573 366935. Full of regulars, good Tuscan home cooking for affordable prices.

APT, Palazzo dei Vescovi, Piazza del Duomo, Pistoia, tel: 0573 21622.
APT, via Lucca Chini 1, Greve in Chianti, tel: 055 8545243.
APT, via Portigiani 3/5, Fiesole, tel: 055 598720.

4
Siena and
Central Tuscany

Roughly in the centre of the Tuscany lies the Medieval town of Siena. Product of a prosperous trading and banking era, Siena manages to marry contemporary life with its backdrop of impressive **Gothic architecture**. This medium-sized town has a compact historic centre, which the visitor can explore by means of its small narrow streets leading from one ancient monument to another. Churches, convents and hospitals are magnificently adorned with **historic frescoes** and are often in a remarkable state of repair.

Beyond the city walls the rolling hills of Tuscany hide other fascinating towns and villages whose existence today is assured not just by tourism but by the vineyards and olive groves for which this famous region is known. Many can be explored within a day. Others merit longer.

Medieval **Monteriggioni** is a short drive from Siena. **San Gimignano** is known for its unusual silhouette punctuated by high towers; the former Etruscan settlement of **Volterra** traces its ancient history; while the small Renaissance town of **Montalcino** comfortably combines a sense of history with the importance of its fine red wine, Brunello.

The Chianti hills, stretching from the province of Florence through that of Siena, produce equally fine **Chianti wines** on the *Colli Senesi* and offer another reason to explore this area, one which also has a large number of interesting little towns, and no shortage of good wineries and restaurants. Art history and gastronomy go hand in hand in the Chianti region.

DON'T MISS

*** **Piazza del Campo:** the focal point of Medieval Siena.
*** **Duomo, Campanile** and **Baptistry, Siena:** lavish examples of Sienese art.
*** **San Gimignano:** Medieval town of towers.
** **Museo dell'Opera del Duomo, Siena:** paintings and sculpture from the Cathedral.
** **Volterra:** an excursion back into the Etruscan lands.
* **Montalcino:** Medieval walled town, superb wines.

Opposite: *The views from Siena's Torre del Mangia are outstanding.*

THE FOUNDING OF SIENA

According to legend, Siena was founded by Ascius and Senius, the sons of Remus, who fled from Rome after their father's murder by his brother Romulus. The spot where they stopped to make sacrifices to Diana and Apollo they called 'Castelsenio' (still the name of a Siena district). The city's colours of black and white are thought to either derive from the colour of the horses ridden by the brothers, or else the smoke from Diana's altar rose white and that from Apollo's black.

SIENA

Possibly another Etruscan settlement that was appropriated by the Romans (legend has it that Remus's sons founded the town – *see* panel, this page), Sena Julia was, however, confirmed as a Roman colony in 1BC. It stagnated until the early Middle Ages, when its trade expanded into northern Europe and it gained a reputation and considerable wealth as a banking centre. Its money lenders soon put it on a par with Florence. However, this similarity degenerated into rivalry as Florence became Guelf, and Siena Ghibelline (*see* page 13). Siena had the upper hand on winning the **Battle of Montaperti** in 1260, but lost it a decade later when defeated by Charles of Anjou and was allied to Florence.

Despite the battles, the 12th and 13th centuries constituted the period of greatest prosperity, both artistic

and economic, for this powerful town, and many of its characteristic brick buildings date from this period. In 1348, plague decimated two thirds of the population and Siena's position declined.

Siena is quite **hilly** and although distances seem minuscule on the map, there may be some climbs from one road to another. The best advice is to leave vehicles in the external parking areas, catch the shuttle bus to the centre, and walk between sights.

Piazza del Campo ***

The Piazza del Campo is probably Italy's most attractive piazza and certainly one of its more unusual. Shaped like an open fan, it is divided by white stone 'spokes' into nine brick-paved sections, to recall the old Council of Nine. Medieval buildings line its perimeter, facing inwards and down the sloping piazza to the magnificent Palazzo del Pubblico at the lower end. Favourite venue for the evening *passegiata* and affluent café-goers,

Central Tuscany

the piazza turns into a wild frenzy for the bi-annual **Palio** (*see* panel, page 74) when 30,000 people cram into its centre as the horse-back riding competitors from 10 of the 17 *contrade* (*see* panel, page 13) battle it out for 30 crucial seconds in a race around the piazza's perimeter.

Opposite: *Overshadowed by the Torre del Mangia, the Palazzo del Pubblico houses a fine collection of early Sienese art.*

Palazzo del Pubblico ★★★

Like a moving finger, the dark shadow of the palazzo's impossibly thin tower, **Torre del Mangia**, and the crenellated silhouette of its roof creep across the piazza as the day passes, changing the fortunes of one fashionable *caffè* in favour of another. This remarkable building was started in 1297 and designed to house civil offices – which in part it still does today. The 102m (335ft) tower was added 40 years later. Open every morning, and also afternoons from March to October, it affords panoramic views of the city after a spiralling climb. The light is at its best either late afternoon or early morning.

Museo Civico ★★★

On the top floor, the palazzo houses the city's Museo Civico (it is open daily), a historic collection of frescoes (by **Simone Martini**, **Ambrogio Lorenzetti**, **Sodoma**, **Spinello Aretino**, **Lippo Vanni** and also, much later, **Domenico Beccafumi**), tapestries and paintings, many

---

MARZOCCO

The figure of the Marzocco, a lion with its paw on the Florentine heraldic lily, soon becomes a familiar one throughout Tuscany. The original was sculpted in 1420 by **Donatello** (and is now in Florence's Bargello) and copies were erected in those towns, including Siena, once held by Medicean Florence.

Above: *Siena's landmark Duomo dates back to the 12th century.*

of which still decorate the walls of this fine building. Look out, in particular, for Simone Martini's vast 1315–21 fresco of the *Maestà* and the beautiful fresco of *Guidoriccio da Fogliano*, traditionally attributed, though now contested, to Martini; and the 1338 fresco cycle, *Allegory of Wise Government* (not surprisingly, a number of Siena's buildings appear in this illustration) and the *Allegory of Evil Government* by **Ambrogio Lorenzetti**, important as one of the first secular subjects depicted in fresco work.

Duomo ***

It is just a short walk via the appropriately named **Via Pellegrini**, Pilgrims' Way, to the Duomo. This extraordinary white, green and pink-striped building, started in the 12th century, was to be incorporated into a far larger church designed in the mid-13th century. However, these ideas were finally scrapped in favour of the original, less grandiose plans, and it was finished 200 years later. Its roots were Romanesque (as is its striped **Campanile**) but much of its execution – the pointed and ogival arches, gabled doorways, pinnacles, and niches with sculpture – is Gothic.

Among the notables to have worked on, or decorated the interior are **Nicola Pisano** (as architect and sculptor), **Jacopo della Quercia**, **Donatello**, **Michelangelo**, **Bernini** and **Pinturicchio**. After getting orientated in this heavily decorated building, look down at the highly original, inlaid marble floor (56 panels by many different artists) then head for Pisano's magnificent carved **pulpit** (1268). Many of the more portable treasures from the Duomo are now displayed in the Museo dell'Opera del Duomo.

Libreria Piccolomini **

Next to the Duomo, this library (open daily in summer, mornings and afternoons in winter) was built to house the library of **Pope Pius II** (Enea Silvio Piccolomini). The Piccolomini emblem (a crescent moon on blue) decorates the floor and friezes, but it is the magnificent cycle of 10 frescoes created by **Pinturicchio** between 1502 and 1509, which has pride of place. Their wonderfully bright, jewel-like colours breathe life into the historic events of Pope Pius II's religious career. The four small statues of saints on the Piccolomini altar are early works by **Michelangelo**. Don't miss the illustrated books, either.

FLORINS

The money men of Central Italy bankrolled western Europe, amassing vast fortunes in the process. The financiers of Florence invented a gold coin weighing 3.5g (1/8 oz) – the florin, the world's first stable currency. The first florin was minted in 1252 and soon became the standard currency throughout the continent.

Museo dell'Opera del Duomo **

The Museum (open daily, shorter hours in winter) housing the treasures of the Duomo offers a fine collection of sculpture. Look for works by **Jacopo della Quercia**, **Giovanni Pisano**, and **Donatello's** beautiful *tondo* of *Mother and Child*. Don't miss the museum's masterpiece: the *Maestà* by **Duccio**. Originally from the cathedral's high altar, this painting was backed by 26 smaller panels depicting scenes from the life of Christ. It was innovative, glistening with gold and vibrating with rich colours, and caused a sensation when it was carried from studio to Duomo.

Battistero San Giovanni *

Behind the Duomo, at a lower level, lies the Baptistry, covered in part by the apse. Its façade was never completed but it is the frescoed vault and the fine hexagonal **font**, topped by a marble tabernacle, that draw the visitors. Among those masters who worked on the *Scenes from the Life of St John the Baptist*, which decorate this superb font, were **Jacopo della Quercia** and **Lorenzo Ghiberti**, as well as **Donatello**.

Below: The Piccolomini Library, built to house Pope Pius II's collection of books, was entirely decorated with colourful frescoes by Pinturicchio and depicts scenes from the Pope's illustrious career.

THE HERMIT AND THE ENSIGN

At via delle Cerchia 50–52 is an ancient marble head of a hermit with a story to tell. In war-torn 1207 a young hermit had a dream in which his patron saint, Andrew, urged him to help the Sienese cause. He followed the military from the Porta all'Arco into battle under their white banner. The next day he was found dead splayed across the white flag which, soaked in blood, had turned red. Not all the flag was bloodied: a diagonal cross stayed white. The cross of St Andrew – a white transversal cross on red – was henceforth adopted as their military insignia.

Ospedale di Santa Maria della Scala **

Located on the Piazza del Duomo, right opposite the western façade of the cathedral, is the 13th-century Ospedale di Santa Maria della Scala, built for the benefit of Medieval pilgrims travelling to Rome via Siena. It ceased functioning as a medical facility in 1996, as parts of it were by then already open to the public. It has superb, restored frescoes depicting, in a very graphic fashion, hospital life in the 15th century. This work was executed around the middle of the century by **Lorenzo Vecchietta** (1412–80), **Domenico Bartolo** (1400–45) and **Priam della Quercia** (1426–67), and today provides social historians with a fine glimpse into the functioning of medicine at that time. There are also works by **Taddeo di Bartolo** and, in the **Cappella del Manto**, by **Beccafumi**. The rather later church of **Santissima Annunziata** has a grandiose apse fresco by 17th-century **Sebastiano Conca**. Part of the hospital complex, it provides a popular venue for local weddings.

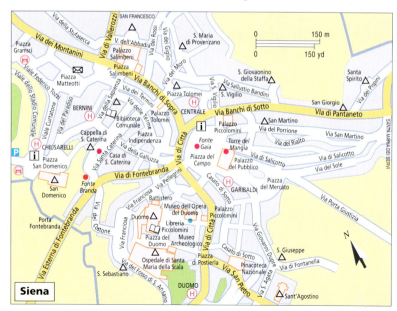

Pinacoteca Nazionale *

This art gallery is located in **Palazzo Buonsignori** (at via San Pietro 29, it is open daily Tuesday to Saturday, mornings only Sunday and Monday) a brick palace from the 15th century. This is the place to make sense of the development of Sienese art from the 13th to 16th centuries. Many of the works are by anonymous painters but it does have some remarkable pieces by **Guido da Siena** (working from early to mid-13th century), **Duccio**, the **Lorenzetti** brothers, **Matteo di Giovanni** (ca. 1430–95), **Vecchietta** (ca. 1412–80), **Beccafumi** (ca. 1484–1551) and **Sodoma** (1477–1549).

Above: St Michael the Archangel, *in colourful 14th-century stained glass.*

More Churches

For the keen walker and art lover, there are four more churches around the cardinal points of the city. In the west, **San Domenico** rises with assurance above the roofs. Despite being dedicated to St Dominic, the legend of **St Catherine** (patron saint of Italy) dominates. It was here that she supposedly saw her ecstatic visions and – although her body is buried in St Maria sopra Minerva, Rome – her head has been returned to her birthplace and is conserved in the church. There is also a contemporary portrait of the Saint, and a cycle of frescoes by **Sodoma**.

Sant'Agostino, situated near the **Botanic Gardens** south of the city, is a Medieval church with a Baroque interior; its treasures include a *Crucifixion* by **Perugino**, as well as works by Sodoma, Matteo di Giovanni and Ambrogio Lorenzetti.

Santa Maria dei Servi, situated on a spur of land in the southeastern part of Siena, affords panoramic views back to the hilltop town centre and boasts a number of 12th–14th-century paintings; and lastly, **San Francesco** with its **Oratorio di San Bernardo**, is the highlight of a visit. The large frescoes in the upper church reflect excellent works by Sienese **Sodoma**, **Beccafumi** and **Girolamo del Pacchia**.

Above: *Monteriggioni's towers sit on its walls like a Medieval coronet.*

Strolling the Streets *

Central Siena is still intrinsically Medieval in form. Wandering through its narrow pedestrian streets, lit by old fashioned lamps, where the buildings are often richly coloured, and the air suffused with a variety of odours (not all pleasant), is to walk in the footsteps of history. Explore the area of small roads, houses cut through by arches, linked by steps and yet more steps, either side of **Via di Città** and **Via Banchi di Sopra**, the commercial pulse of this ancient town. The latter curves around to the 14th-century **Piazza Salimbeni**, a fine piazza named for the old **Palazzo** in which the banking family Salimbeni once lived. For vernacular architecture, investigate **Via del Capitano** and also **Via della Galluzza** with its arches. This area is very crowded with tourists but, moving outwards, the curious will soon stroll into neighbourhood streets where *alimentari*, grocery shops, serve the needs of the local community rather than the souvenir-hungry tourist.

EXCURSIONS NORTHWEST OF SIENA

It is only 15km (nearly 10 miles) to **Monteriggioni**, a gem of a Medieval town, and another 28km (nearly 18 miles) further, via the ancient hilltop settlement of **Colle di Val d'Elsa**, to one of Italy's quirkiest and most endearing Medieval towns, **San Gimignano**.

CHIANTI CLASSICO

Chianti Classico, a *DOCG* (*Denominazione di Origine Controllata e Garantita*) labelled wine, is only produced on some 7000ha (nearly 17,000 acres) around Greve, Gaiole and Castellina in Chianti, and Barberino Val d'Elsa. Wine lovers should be sure to visit Siena's **Enoteca Italiana**, Fortezza Medicea 1, Siena, tel: 0577 288497, to taste and learn more about Italian wines and in particular the local Chianti.

Monteriggioni **

The forbidding stone walls of Monteriggioni sit, like a fancy coronet, around the small village peaking into 14 sentinel towers. It is as one imagines a Medieval walled town should be, and is very well preserved. Walk through its tiny centre – from one town gate to the other takes less than five minutes – and look at the attractive houses and the Romanesque church. This is the kind of place to come on a warm evening, linger in the piazza and enjoy an apéritif under the starry night sky.

The road onward passes a turning for the **Abbadia Isola**, an abbey to the west of Monteriggioni started in 1001 but fortified only some 300 years later by the Sienese.

Colle di Val d'Elsa *

People often overlook this old town in their haste to reach the better-known San Gimignano. Stop en route and explore the more interesting upper town. The renovated **Duomo** on the paved Piazza del Duomo defines the heart of Colle Alta (upper Colle). It is a 17th-century building with a stately neo-Classical façade which updated its original Romanesque form. Opposite the Duomo lie the **Palazzo del Vescovo**, the Bishop's Palace, and the restored 14th-century **Palazzo Pretorio**, now home to the **Museo Archeologico** (open Tuesday to Sunday, late mornings and late afternoons in summer, and afternoons only in winter). The museum displays local finds, including some interesting items from Etruscan tombs.

The **Museo Civico d'Arte Sacra** (open during the summer months from Tuesday to Sunday, mornings and afternoons, and in winter only on Saturday mornings and afternoons) offers paintings and statues by talented but lesser known Tuscan artists, as well as other religious artifacts.

Below: *A Medieval town just a few minutes from Siena, Colle di Val d'Elsa offers the tourist much of historical interest.*

SAN GIMIGNANO

Monteriggioni may well have been noted for the fine state of its towers, but San Gimignano, 42km (26 miles) from Siena, also boasts a perpendicular profile.

Long before you arrive at San Gimignano you will see its 14 famous towers. There were once 72 of them. During the rivalry between Guelfs and Ghibellines, San Gimignano was Guelf (**Dante** visited to argue the cause) and ultimately sided with Florence during the feuds between Siena and Florence. It was then that the towers were erected by wealthy families to protect themselves from opposing factions.

What you see today is distinctly Medieval, despite Etruscan and Roman roots – narrow streets, warm brick and stone walls, old churches, city gates and terracotta tiled roofs rising above a landscape of olive groves and vineyards (producing San Gimignano's white *Vernaccia* wine). Tourism has unfortunately discovered this appealing small town and it gets terribly crowded during the summer season. Visitors should park their cars outside town and take a leisurely stroll through its ancient walls, to discover its monuments, cafés and restaurants, not forgetting the many souvenir shops selling local *Vernaccia* wines, **pottery** and decoratively packaged **foodstuffs**.

Below: *The ancient well in San Gimignano is a favourite gathering spot.*

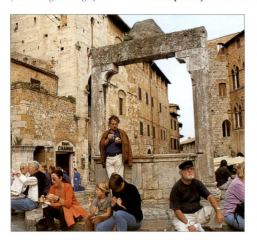

Collegiata di Santa Maria Assunta ***

Once the town's cathedral (though demoted when San Gimignano was no longer a bishopric), this austere, 12th-century Romanesque building was enlarged in the 1460s by the architect and sculptor **Giuliano da Maiano**. It is the frescoes which bring people here: the interior is lavishly decorated with stories of saints, biblical episodes and of the local saint, Santa Fina.

In the right-hand aisle, as you enter, you will see the incomplete cycle of 14th-century frescoes depicting the *Life of Christ*, believed to be by **Barna da Siena**, an artist from the studio of Simone Martini. It is said that he died as a result of falling from his scaffolding, leaving the massive frescoes unfinished. The *Old Testament* on the north wall, opposite, was painted by **Bartolo di Fredi**.

Above: *San Gimignano once boasted over 70 towers. Today some 14 still stand.*

The **Cappella di Santa Fina** was created in 1468 by **Giuliano da Maiano** to honour the local girl, Serafina di Ciardi, who died at the age of 16 and who was later beatified. It was decorated by **Domenico Ghirlandaio** when he was only 25 years old. This Florentine artist was to become *the* master of fresco later in life. The **Museo d'Arte Sacra** (open daily in summer; open mornings and afternoons, except Monday, in winter), adjacent to the Collegiata, houses a number of the treasures from the Collegiata as well as some fine Etruscan artifacts.

If you wander past the late 13th-century Palazzo del Popolo, which encloses the **Museo Civico** (open during the same hours as the Museo d'Arte Sacra above), you will come across an alley leading to the **Piazza della Cisterna**, named for the well in its centre – a pretty piazza paved in brick (similar to the nearby **Piazza Pecori**) and laid out in a traditional herringbone design. Don't overlook the **Benozzo Gozzoli** frescoes in **San Agostino**, a renovated church in the peaceful Piazza San Agostino, at the northern end of town.

MUSEO DELLA TORTURA

Not for the squeamish (but ideal for world-weary adolescents), the Torture Museum in San Gimignano is one of its newer attractions. It features ancient torture contraptions from varying epoques of history. The exhibits have been collected from all over Italy and also include documents relating to torture and the death sentence, and devices used by the Inquisition. Open daily, via del Castello 1–3, tel: 0577 942243.

Above: *Detail from a 2300-year-old Etruscan urn in the Guarnacci Museum, Volterra.*

Volterra **

This ancient town dates back to the Stone Age although it is better known for its Etruscan and Roman remains. It was one of Etruria's most prosperous towns before the Romans usurped its power. The rather sober Volterra abuts two totally different landscapes: the rounded contours of agricultural land of the north and the craggy, crumbly escarpments to the west.

Chronologically the first site to visit is **Porta all'Arco**, the Etruscan arch on the western side of town, built in the 4th century BC; then a walk up to the **Porta San Felice** and its surrounding area will reveal a mishmash of Etruscan, Roman and Medieval architecture.

For more Etruscan sights, visit the **Museo Etrusco Guarnacci** at Via Don Minzoni (it is open daily). This museum provides a fine history of Etruscan art from the 8th to the 2nd century BC. Be sure to look out for the **alabaster work** (for which Volterra is still renowned) and also the **funerary urns**.

The town's Roman remains comprise the ruins of a small **theatre** nestling beyond the northern walls of town. Its Medieval heart is the **Piazza San Giovanni**, where the **Duomo**, **Palazzo Pretorio** and **Palazzo dei Priori** stand. The Duomo has, in the Addolorata Chapel, a *Procession of the Magi* by **Benozzo Gozzoli**. The small octagonal building situated beside the stone Duomo is the 13th-century **Battistero** (baptistry) decorated, like other Pisa-influenced churches, with those familiar green and white marbles.

Colli Senesi

The centre of the Chianti area, this is as accessible from Siena as it is from Florence. For information on the *Colli Fiorentini*, *see* page 66.

**WHERE TO SEE
ETRUSCAN REMAINS**

• **Florence:**
Museo Archeologico
• **Volterra:**
Museo Etrusco Guarnacci
• **Arezzo:**
Museo Archeologico
• **Cortona:**
Museo dell'Accademia Etrusca
• **Colle di Val d'Elsa:**
Museo Archeologico
• **San Gimignano:**
Museo d'Arte Sacra
• **Pistoia:**
Palazzo dei Vescovi
• **San Appiano:**
Antiquarium
• **Sovana:**
Etruscan tombs

Via Chiantigiana, leading north from Siena towards Florence, passes through **Castellina in Chianti**, a pleasant 13th-century walled town with an unusual vaulted street, **Via delle Volte**, which follows the contours of the town walls. Castellina sits in a vulnerable position between the Florentine and Sienese territories and passed from side to side as one city gained territory over the other. Along with Radda and Gaiole, Castellina formed part of the *Lega di Chianti*, the **Chianti League**, (*see* panel, this page).

Radda in Chianti had a similar fate. Another Medieval village built on former Etruscan foundations, it assumed the position of the premier castle in the Chianti League.

The beautiful monastic complex at Coltibuono, **La Badia a Coltibuono**, boasts a fortified 11th-century church amid other buildings associated with this abbey and presides over a green landscape of pine and oak trees.

Amid more perfect Tuscan countryside lies the town of **Gaiole in Chianti**, another member of the League. Further to the south you'll see the castle at **Meleto**, a meticulously restored stronghold dating originally from the 12th century, which remains privately owned.

The castle at **Brolio**, however, is open to visitors (daily, mornings and afternoons, except in winter). A magnificent 15th-century castellated building, it is owned by the well-known noble family (and wine producer), Ricasoli.

> ### IL GALLO NERO
>
> Along with Radda and Gaiole, Castellina formed part of the *Lega di Chianti*, the **Chianti League**, a 13th-century military alliance to deal with Siena's ever-present expansionist efforts. The emblem of this union was the Black Rooster, the *Gallo Nero*. Today the *Gallo Nero* has less belligerent connotations. It is on a label of **Chianti Classico** wine.

Below: *The castle at Brolio is one of Tuscany's most picturesque. Owned by the Ricasoli family, it is open to the public.*

Below: *The small and
very attractive town of
Buonconvento is often
overlooked by tourists.*

Excursions South of Siena

Small fortified villages and the remains of 12th-century
abbeys are found south of Siena in a pretty landscape of
wheat and sunflowers draped over undulating hills,
sometimes clothed with chestnut and oak forests. Unlike
northern Tuscany, there are noticeably fewer tourists here.

Buonconvento *

This small, red-brick village, at the confluence of two
rivers, is enclosed within 14th-century brick walls. Its
principal street offers some fine period houses and the
Palazzo Pretorio. Take a quick look at the church of
SS Pietro e Paolo, rebuilt with a Jesuit façade. If your
interests take in early religious art, be sure to visit the
Museo d'Arte Sacra della Val d'Arbia (open Tuesday to
Sunday, mornings and afternoons). It contains various
12th–15th-century items from local churches.

Abbazia di Monte Oliveto Maggiore **

In tranquil countryside, the Abbey of Monte Oliveto
Maggiore (open daily, mornings and afternoons) is just
8km (5 miles) from Buonconvento. It dates from the early
14th century and housed a breakaway branch of the
Benedictine order, the Olivetans. On entering, a *Madonna
and Child* by **Giovanni della Robbia** appears in a niche,
complemented by a *St Benedict* opposite. The monastery
is renowned for its fresco cycle of the life of St Benedict,
painted by **Luca Signorelli** and finished by **Sodoma**, in the
mid-15th-century cloister.
Signorelli's figures stand out
for their powerful muscular
bodies while Sodoma's pref-
erence seems to have been
for the landscape details.

Abbazia San Galgano *

Ruins are what remains of
this abbey, but they are
impressive. It was built in
the mid-13th century by the

Left: *Dropping away from the hilltop town of Montalcino are the vineyards that produce one of Italy's most prized red wines, Brunello di Montalcino.*

Cistercians and in the complex is their church, reputed to be the earliest Gothic church in Tuscany. St Galgano, born into a wealthy Sienese family but called to the Church, spent his last days in prayer, at a small domed hermitage just a couple of hundred metres from the abbey.

Montalcino *

A provincial road heads 15km (10 miles) southwards from Buonconvento and winds up to the hilltop town of Montalcino. There are two reasons to visit this attractive town – its **Medieval brick walls** and its **wine**.

Rising 564m (1880ft) above the valley and heavily fortified, the village of Montalcino was a safe haven in Medieval times, and was often used as a refuge for the Sienese. A **fortress**, the 14th-century church of **Sant'Agostino** (with its attached museum of sacred arts, open daily, mornings and afternoons, except Monday) and the 17th-century **Madonna di Soccorso**, a church popular with pilgrims, are all worth visiting.

The **Brunello di Montalcino**, made entirely with the Sangiovese cultivar, is one of the country's 20-odd wines which carry the label *DOCG* (*Denominazione di Origine Controllata e Garantita*) the highest guarantee of a quality wine. Along with the best Chiantis, Brunello is considered one of Tuscany's finest wines. Wine buffs should look out for the **Enoteca Fortezza**, in the converted 14th-century castle, or the pleasant **Caffè Fiaschetteria Italiana** in Piazza del Popolo, where wine of the region is available for tasting and purchase.

ABBAZIA DI SANT'ANTIMO

Not far from Montalcino and in a pastoral landscape tidied up with neat rows of olive trees, lies the dignified Abbey of Sant'Antimo. It was originally constructed in the 9th century, and its church in the 12th, by the Cistercians. Although the church is in a fairly good state of repair, the monastic buildings have fared less well. Services are still celebrated in the somewhat austere church.

Siena and Central Tuscany at a Glance

BEST TIMES TO VISIT

Like Florence, Siena and its nearby towns get crowded in **summer** when many festivals (like the famous Palio) take place. **Autumn** and **spring** are delightful in the town, and the countryside is at its best. **Winter** can be quite cold and rainy, but the sites are easier to visit. Note that the winter opening hours are often shorter than in summer. A number of hotels are not open in winter, especially from Christmas to March. Ring or fax ahead to check. Some restaurants are also closed during winter.

GETTING THERE

Use the **airports** at either Pisa or Florence (for full details *see* Travel Tips, page 122) and then travel southwards by **rail** or **road**. Regular **trains** run between Florence and Siena, a journey time of some 94 minutes. For travellers coming from Rome, there are frequent railway connections from the capital (changing at Chiusi or Grosseto) with a travel time of between 2.5 and 4 hours. Details of rail services throughout Italy on website: www.fs-on-line.it **Buses** connect the railway station, just out of town, with the modern centre of Siena, near Piazza del Campo. However, the easiest way to explore is by **car**. Siena is linked with Florence by the fast **superstrada**,which takes almost an

hour. SITA **bus** services from Florence are also frequent. Onward services go to Grosseto. Those driving should note that many historic town centres are closed to traffic. In Siena, cars must be left on the outskirts of town in parking areas, and local buses ferry tourists to the town centre.

GETTING AROUND

Within each town, nothing is easier than **walking**, once the car is safely parked. Between sites, **car** travel is the easiest and allows one to explore the back roads. **Rail** is of limited use for exploring the area. However, **bus** services offered by Lazzi and SITA link the major towns mentioned with Siena, or with Florence. Alternatively, tours (*see* Useful Contacts, page 87) offered by Sienese travel agents will take the visitor to various points of interest in the area.

WHERE TO STAY

LUXURY
Park Hotel Siena, via Marciano 18, Siena, tel: 0577 44803, fax: 0577 49020, website: www.thecharminghotels.com Beautiful outlook, finest comfort, north of *centro storico*. Excellent restaurant, L'Olivo.
Hotel Garden, via Custoza 2, Siena, tel: 0577 47056, fax: 0577 46050, website: www.gardenhotel.it/compgarden Just 2km north of centre, in mature parkland. Ask for rooms in original 18th-century villa.

Relais Santa Chiara, via Matteotti 15, località Santa Chiara, San Gimignano, tel: 0577 940701, fax: 0577 942096. Mid-sized hotel just outside town centre, views over countryside and garden.
Castello di Spaltenna, via Spaltenna 13, Gaiole in Chianti, tel: 0577 749483, fax: 0577 749269. Great setting overlooking hills. The hotel is in a 13th-century monastery and has an excellent restaurant.

MID-RANGE
Castagneto, via dei Cappuccini 39, Siena, tel: 0577 45103, fax: 0577 283266. Delightful small hotel with view to the city and the surrounding hills. Closed in winter.
Salivolpi, via Fiorentina 89, Castellina in Chianti, tel: 0577 740484, fax: 0577 740998. In converted stone farmhouses, this is a fine hotel with pleasant grounds.
Hotel Monteriggioni, via 1 Maggio 4, Monteriggioni, tel: 0577 305009, fax: 0577 305011. Small hotel bordering city walls. Tasteful and pleasant.
San Lino, via San Lino 26, Volterra, tel: 0588 85250, fax: 0588 80620. Within the city walls (no parking), a pleasant medium-sized hotel in former convent. Closed in winter.
Villa Rioddi, località Rioddi, Volterra, tel: 0588 88053, fax: 0588 88074. Modernized 15th-century villa, situated just outside Volterra. Closed between January and March.

Siena and Central Tuscany at a Glance

BUDGET

Albergo Chiusarelli, via Curtatone 15, Siena, tel: 0577 280562, fax: 0577 271177. Beside San Domenico, a quiet hotel with garden. There is parking nearby.

Locanda Il Pino, via Cellolese 4, San Gimignano, tel: 0577 940415. Pleasant accommodation, clean rooms.

WHERE TO EAT

LUXURY

Antica Trattoria Botteganova, via Chiantigiana 29, Siena, tel: 0577 284230. This is a well-respected restaurant situated just outside the centre, on the Montevarchi route. Michelin-rated cuisine.

Vignale, via XX Settembre 23, Radda in Chianti, tel: 0577 738094. Excellent Tuscan fare. Reservations are essential. Closed mid-winter.

Arnolfo, via XX Settembre 50, Colle di Val d'Elsa, tel: 0577 920549. One of Tuscany's best restaurants and worth the reservation. Lovely view of the hills from the terrace. It also has four guest rooms.

Castello di Spaltenna, Gaiole in Chianti, *see* Where to Stay.

MID-RANGE

Al Marsili, via del Castoro 3, Siena, tel: 0577 47154. Situated at a smart address, this restaurant has a good menu and excellent wine list.

Osteria Le Logge, via del Porrione 33, Siena, tel: 0577 48013. A centrally located restaurant, well decorated and offering consistently good Tuscan cuisine.

Poggio Antico, on Poggio Antico estates, approximately 4km (2.5 miles) southwest of Montalcino, towards Sant'Angelo in Colle, tel: 0577 849200. A farm-style restaurant known for its delicious Tuscan cooking.

Il Pozzo, piazza Roma 2, Monteriggioni, tel: 0577 304127. An excellent restaurant located in this increasingly popular town.

Antica Trattoria La Torre, Piazza del Comune, Castellina in Chianti, tel: 0577 740236. This family-run trattoria has a rustic ambience. It offers good, hearty fare as well as some excellent wines.

Restaurant Badia a Coltibuono, Badia a Coltibuono, tel: 0577 749424. A well-known and popular restaurant with excellent local cuisine.

Al Brunello di Montalcino, località Bellaria, near Montalcino, tel: 0577 849304. This excellent restaurant is a fine place to sample the local wines accompanied by a first-rate meal.

Ristorante Bar Etruria, piazza dei Priori 6/8, Volterra, tel: 0588 86064. Attractive rustic setting, good local food and very central.

BUDGET

Trattoria la Torre, via Salicotto 7, Siena, tel: 0577 287548. A small restaurant serving the typical, good Tuscan fare that attracts both locals and tourists.

Ristorante Il Pino, via San Matteo 102, San Gimignano, tel: 0577 940415. Small restaurant featuring home cooking. Simple but good.

SHOPPING

Apart from the vast selection of Chianti wines, the olive oils and wine vinegars in this region are also excellent. San Gimignano is known for its pretty pottery. Volterra has a tradition of producing alabaster. Siena also has a reputation for good cakes, such as the *panforte*. As a smart provincial town, Siena has a fine choice of shops offering fashion goods. Leather bags and shoes, woollens and other items of clothing are all good buys.

USEFUL CONTACTS

Centro Servizi Informazioni Turistiche, piazza del Campo 56, Siena, tel: 0577 280551.

APT, piazza Duomo 1, San Gimignano, tel: 0577 940008.

APT, piazza dei Priori 20, Volterra, tel: 0588 87257.

Ufficio Turistico Communale, costa del Municipio 8, Montalcino, tel: 0577 849331.

5
Southeastern Tuscany

It used to be a long and difficult journey from Florence to the hills of Eastern Tuscany. Although it has become much easier today, thanks to fast roads slicing through the mountains, most visitors still favour the large and more publicized towns to the west.

Yet eastwards, beyond the dales and valleys of the Chianti Hills, lies another vision of Tuscany – perhaps more authentic, and certainly less touched by tourism. Within this area of Tuscany, in an undulating landscape of olives, vines and dark cypress trees, there are plenty of small towns, all easily accessible, and each one with a link to the past.

The hilltown of **Arezzo** has an illustrious history dating back to the Etruscans, and gave birth to three notable sons. Its *centro storico* boasts among others, the marvellous fresco cycle by Piero della Francesca, who came from **Sansepolcro**, some 40km (25 miles) away. **Cortona**, one of the oldest cities in Tuscany, has Etruscan roots and an important Renaissance centre.

To the south, the small town of **Montepulciano** charms even the most jaded of tourists. So, too, the well-designed town of **Pienza**. And in this area, less scored by roads but rising to Tuscany's highest peak, **Mount Amiata**, there are old abbeys, Medieval towers and Etruscan tombs all hidden within a landscape that comes straight out of a Gozzoli or della Francesca painting.

Further afield, excursions into Tuscany's neighbouring province (Umbria) take the visitor to two of Italy's most historic towns: **Assisi** and **Perugia**.

DON'T MISS

*** Arezzo: see Piero della Francesca's fresco cycle.
** Camaldoli: an ancient hermitage and Carthusian monastery.
** Pienza: a Renaissance gem with integral town planning.
** Montepulciano: for its hilltop town and wines.
* Cortona: visit the Renaissance church of Santa Maria del Calcinaio.

Opposite: *Just outside the town of Montepulciano lies the beautiful Tempio di San Biagio.*

AREZZO

When you first see it, perched on a small incline rising above fertile agricultural land, Arezzo is not a particularly attractive modern town. But within its contemporary shell it has an old centre which attests to its prosperous past, both in Etruscan (it was known for its unique pottery) and Renaissance times. Arezzo was also the birthplace of **Petrarch**, the artist **Spinello Aretino**, and the architect **Giorgio Vasari**. But it is better known for one of the most remarkable fresco cycles of the Renaissance: **Piero della Francesca**'s *Legend of the True Cross*, worth the journey alone.

In the northern part of the town, two churches merit a visit. The first is **San Domenico** with a lovely *Crucifix*, and the second is the **Duomo**, a building with an unappealing exterior that belies its fine interior.

Piazza Grande **

This is the town's focal point, a large, heavily sloping piazza, on the northern side of the old walled town. It has a fine Medieval feel thanks to its remaining crenellated towers, the most attractive being Torre dei Cofani and Lappoli, its narrow, old houses and views of the lovely, Romanesque, Santa Maria della Pieve. Arezzo was one of the 12 towns in the *Lega di Chianti* (*see* page 83) and during those years the town prospered and many fine houses were built. The piazza is also home to the monthly **Antiques Fair**, a popular date with lovers of bric-a-brac and furniture, and the riotous annual joust, **Giostra del Saracino**, end August, beginning September.

Santa Maria della Pieve **

This is one of the most attractive Romanesque churches in Tuscany – the rounded apse with its delightful double-storey arcade, and its noble campanile, built in 1330, are excellent examples of this 12th-century style and possibly executed by a Pisan or Lucchese architect. Giorgio Vasari (*see* panel, this page) was the architect responsible for the 16th-century alterations to Santa Maria.

Next to the church, have a look at the **Palazzo della Fraternità dei Laici**, a sturdy palace topped with three bells, built between the 14th and 16th centuries for a lay confraternity and, along the northeastern side, the **Loggia** (1573), also designed by Vasari. **Vasari's house**, in Via XX Settembre, is also open to visitors. He built and decorated much of it himself. The dignified stone house once occupied by **Petrarch**, via dell'Orto 28, is now the seat of the Petrarch Academy. It, too, may be visited.

The eclectic **Museo Statale d'Arte Medioevale e Moderna**, (corner Via Garibaldi and Via San Lorentino, open daily; Sunday mornings only) is housed in 15th-century **Palazzo Bruni Ciocchi** and exhibits paintings, sculpture and maiolica (*see* panel, page 79).

Those interested in Arezzo's Etruscan and Roman past would do well to head for the **Museo Archeologico** (open mornings only) overlooking the Roman amphitheatre, and have a look at the items discovered in Etruscan graves, and the fine collection of Aretine vases for which the city was noted, produced in Arezzo between the 1st century BC and the 1st century AD.

GIORGIO VASARI (1511–74)

A true Renaissance man (born in Arezzo, trained in Florence), Giorgio Vasari was a painter, architect and impresario. His famous book, *Le Vite de' più eccellenti Pittori, Scultori et Architetti Italiani*, published in 1550, was republished in 1568 and, translated as **Lives of the Artists**, is probably the single most important art historical document ever published. It relates the rivalry and commissions of 20 of the best Gothic and Renaissance artists (culminating in Michelangelo, his hero) and thanks to his description art historians have been able to unravel the complex relations of the art world 600 years ago.

Opposite *Arezzo's Piazza Grande has a Medieval feel.*
Below: *Vasari's Loggia houses an Arezzo café.*

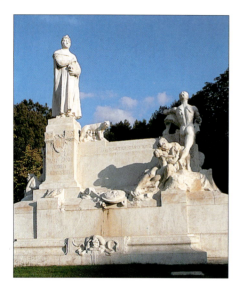

Above: *The Petrarch Monument in Arezzo.*

San Francesco ***

The best is left till last. Around 1450 **Piero della Francesca** was invited to complete the cycle of frescoes depicting the *Legend of the True Cross*, which had been commissioned by the Bacci family for the apse walls of San Francesco. The work was awarded to **Bicci di Lorenzo**. However, de Lorenzo left Arezzo having hardly started and it fell to Piero to finish the œuvre. In doing so he produced one of the greatest fresco cycles in Italy. Tickets should be bought in advance as numbers of visitors are restricted.

Carefully restored, this work is full of innovative ways to depict the story (taken from the 13th-century *Golden Legend*) of St Helena who brought a fragment of Christ's cross to Italy, of her son Emperor Constantine's conversion to Christianity, and of the miraculous powers of the cross. A number of aspects of the work attest to Piero's close observation of nature, his understanding of mathematics and his scholarship in perspective: the way he has painted the clothes of the women around the **Queen of Sheba**; the lifelike **portraits** of classical figures and contemporary **personalities**; the correct foreshortening of the angel in the dark sky (in the night scene with slumbering Constantine); the use of light for modelling; the beautiful and delicate colour coordination.

There are remains of other frescoes in this rather austere Gothic church. Local artist **Spinello Aretino** produced the *Annunciation* which is located on the right-hand side of the aisle.

The Gothic **Duomo** contains, among many other interesting works, a lovely fresco by Piero, the *Santa Maria Magdalena*, and magnificent stained-glass windows by a 15th-century French glassmaker.

Excursions **

Sansepolcro, some 39km (25 miles) from Arezzo, was the birthplace of **Piero della Francesca**. It owes its name to the two pilgrims who, in the 10th century, returned from the Holy Land with relics from the *Santo Sepolcro*, the Holy Sepulchre, around which a chapel was created and, soon, a village was born. It was quite a prosperous Medieval town which **Piazza Torre di Berta**, the large central piazza, still reflects. More historic buildings line **Via XX Settembre**. Though Piero della Francesca is more often associated with Arezzo, he was born here to a humble shoemaker, worked part of his life and finally died here in 1492. The **Museo Civico** (via Aggiunti 65, open mornings and afternoons) has a number of his, and other artists', excellent works.

The N71 north from Arezzo to **Parco Nazionale delle Foreste Casentinesi, Monte Falterona e Campigna** passes a couple of interesting towns. The first of these is **Bibbiena** and the second **Poppi**. From here it is quite a hilly but

Southeastern Tuscany

lovely drive to the isolated Carthusian monastery of **Camaldoli**, founded in 1016 by St Romuald, a breakaway Benedictine monk. A short distance further up through the old, deciduous forests of **Casentino**, you will come to **Camaldoli Hermitage**. Founded in 1012 by St Romuald, it is best known for its curious monastic cells laid out like a village.

Opposite: The church of Santa Maria del Calcinaio lies just outside Cortona.

CORTONA

In early history, the hilltop site of Cortona was an Etruscan *lucumonia*. It passed into Roman hands but later fell into decline due to malaria in the low, swampy areas below the town. By the *trecento*, Cortona was back on the map and by the *quattrocento*, expanding. Little has changed since then, except for the planting of more **olive groves**, making the town an attractive place to explore, with a few interesting sights. Cortona was also the birthplace of three eminent Tuscan artists: the talented Renaissance painter, **Luca Signorelli** (ca. 1441–1523), Baroque fresco master, **Pietro (Berrettini) da Cortona** (1596–1669), and Futurist painter, **Gino Severini** (1883–1966).

Museo dell'Accademia Etrusca *

As befits an Etruscan town, this museum (open Tuesday to Sunday, mornings and afternoons) displays a good collection of statues, ceramics and some fine bronzes. There are also a number of 14th- to 17th-century paintings, including works by **Signorelli** and **Pietro da Cortona**.

Museo Diocesano *

Housed in the former Jesuit church, this eclectic collection comprises paintings (an *Annunciation* by **Fra Angelico**, a *Deposition* by **Signorelli**, cartoon plans for a series of mosaics by **Severini**) and a magnificent 16th-century wooden ceiling.

Santa Maria del Calcinaio **

This is a beautiful Renaissance church 3km (nearly 2 miles), south of Cortona. Built by **Francesco di Giorgio Martini** in 1485, with unusually dark stone, it is in the form of a Latin cross, mounted by a raised cupola. In contrast, the interior is much lighter and although the church hasn't weathered well, it is still impressive.

EXCURSIONS FROM CORTONA

Although not part of Tuscany, over the border in Umbria, beyond Lake Trasimeno, are two of Italy's most famous and interesting towns, Perugia and Assisi, and they are both accessible from Cortona.

Lago di Trasimeno *

This is central Italy's largest lake and is located about halfway between Cortona and Perugia. It is an attractive lake, surrounded by vineyards and olive groves and rimmed with hills topped with old *castelli*, but blighted by the *autostrada del sole* which skirts its northern shores. In distant days it was the scene of a bloody battle between the Carthaginians, led by Hannibal, and the Romans, led by Flaminius (Hannibal vanquished the Romans). Boats will take visitors across to **Isola Maggiore**, one-time retreat of St Francis of Assisi.

Perugia ***

Perugia is one of central Italy's most visited cities and one which attracts plenty of young people to

> **BEST BOVINE**
>
> A huge T-bone steak, *Bistecca Fiorentina*, will be delivered to your table, hot and so rare its will still be oozing blood. This is the way Florentines eat their steak and though you can always send it back for a bit more grilling, it really is the most tasty served this way. The steak is the product of the **Calvana** breed of cow, an animal which has been around for over 2200 years. The white Calvana is believed to have had Umbro-Etruscan origins and is indigenous to the Val di Chiana.

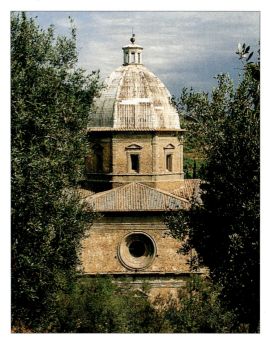

GIOTTO (CA. 1266–1337)

A revolutionary artist, Giotto forsook the stylized Byzantine forms and colouring for a new realism which art had not yet witnessed and which radically influenced the young artists of the day. He gave his frescoed and painted figures **form** and **plasticity**, using gentle colours. For this breakaway attitude we now consider him the father of modern painting. His most impressive works are in the **Arena Chapel** in Padua; the frescoes for **San Francesco**, Assisi (though modern thinking does not attribute the actual execution to this Florentine master); the Bardi and Peruzzi Chapels in **Santa Croce**, Florence, and a painted wooden crucifix in **Santa Maria Novella**, Florence, which is attributed to him. For his abilities, he was appointed supervisor of **Florence Cathedral** in 1334.

its **language schools**. It is the capital of the province of the same name. Its history goes back to Etruscan days when it was a *lucumonia*, one of the 12 city-states forming the Etruscan federation in the 7th century BC. The **City walls** still date from this era. The Romans took it in the fourth century BC. The many **Medieval buildings** attest to a period of expansion in the 11th–14th centuries. In the 15th century it was incorporated into the papal states.

Perugia's fame also rests with the Renaissance artists who started their careers here. **Perugino** (1445–1523) was the most influential, teaching the young **Raphael** (1483–1520) and the master of fresco, **Pinturicchio** (1454–1518).

Highlight of a visit to this city is **Piazza Quattro Novembre**. The large 13th-century fountain, **Fontana Maggiore**, which graces this piazza, boasts a fine collection of sculpted friezes by **Nicola Pisano** and his son, **Giovanni**. The **Palazzo dei Priori**, a fine but rather sober 13th-century palace, houses the excellent **Galleria Nazionale dell'Umbria**, a magnificent collection of Umbrian painting and sculpture.

The large **Gothic cathedral**, flanking onto the piazza, boasts a fine Baroque portal on its façade. Another impressive church is the **Oratorio di San Bernadino**, with its fine façade by Agostino di Duccio. Don't miss, either, the lovely frescoes by Perugino in the **Collegio del Cambio**, the moneychangers' guildhouse.

Assisi ***

One of the most touristy towns in all Italy, Assisi remains, despite its recent catastrophic earthquake, one of the most impressive. The serenity one associates with St Francis somehow permeates the town's light-coloured walls and narrow streets to imbue it with a similar tranquillity. Assisi is at its best in winter, when it is less crowded. St Francis was born here in 1182, established the Franciscan Order in 1210 and died in 1226.

The most important sight here is the **Basilica di San Francesco**, two separate buildings known as the **Lower** and **Upper Basilica**, both consecrated in 1253 and now much restored after the 1997 earthquakes. The Lower Basilica is decorated with fading 13th- and 14th-century frescoes and paintings by, among others, **Simone Martini**, **Pietro Lorenzetti** and **Cimabue**. The Upper Basilica houses a fine Cimabue crucifix, the famous and extensive fresco cycle depicting the life of St Francis, designed by **Giotto** but perhaps not actually executed by his hand, and also some frescoes attributed to **Pietro Cavallini**. St Francis's tomb is in the crypt of the lower church.

Opposite: *Assisi stands on a hillside affording panoramic views to the west.*
Below: *The austere façade of the Basilica di San Francesco, Assisi.*

Other buildings not to be missed include the 13th-century church of **Santa Chiara**, at the other end of Assisi, decorated with Giottoesque frescoes, and the **Eremo dei Carceri**, some 4km (2.5 miles) from Assisi, where St Francis and his followers used to retreat. Today the spot is much the same as the saint must have found it around 800 years ago. A visit to the **Convento di San Damiano** is likewise interesting for it was constructed at the place where the cross was supposed to have spoken to young Francis, the event which led to his conversion. It too, is a pleasant, peaceful place.

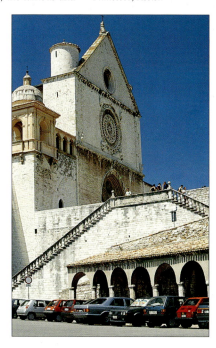

MONTEPULCIANO

There are two very good reasons to encourage the visitor to cross the Val di Chiana valley and climb to the well-preserved and prosperous Renaissance town of Montepulciano: the works of the sculptor-architect Antonio da Sangallo il Vecchio (the elder of the two da Sangallos) which grace the town, and also a local wine, *vino nobile di Montepulciano*.

Centro Storico ★

The centre of the town focuses on the **Piazza Grande**, slightly theatrical in feel, from which the main streets – Via Ricci and Via Voltaia nel Corso – stretch northwards. The piazza is dominated by the broad, unfinished façade of the late 16th-century **Duomo** (Ippolito Scalza was the architect). Inside, there are the scattered remains of a Michelozzo-designed tomb for Bartolomeo Aragazzi, secretary to Pope Martin V; a dazzling Taddeo di Bartolo tryptich (1401); and a terracotta by Luca della Robbia (more terracottas by Luca's nephew, Andrea, are displayed in the **Museo Civico**, Via Ricci, along with some interesting Etruscan exhibits).

Palazzo del Capitano del Popolo is an extensively remodelled Gothic palace occupying a piazza-front location. Abutting this palace is the massive **Palazzo Tarugi** and the delightful **Pozzo de' Griffi e de' Leoni**, a well, in front. Both these structures are the work of architect Antonio da Sangallo the Elder, who also designed but did not finish the **Palazzo Contucci** on the east side of the piazza. The very impressive **Palazzo Comunale**, situated directly opposite Palazzo Contucci on the west side of Piazza Grande, offers a stunning panorama from its tower.

Below: *Montepulciano, in central Tuscany, has a rich architectural heritage.*

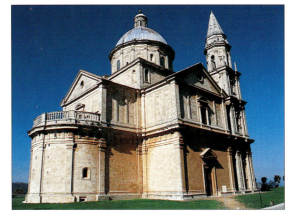

Along Via di Gracciano, the same talented architect designed the **Palazzo Cocconi** and could also possibly have been responsible for the elegant **Palazzo Cervini**, constructed for Riccardo Cervini who, as Marcellus II, assumed the pontificiate for the last 21 days of his life.

On the northern extremity of town, through the historic **Porto al Prado** and just before the 14th-century church to local saint, Sant'Agnese, Antonio da Sangallo the Elder designed the ramparts to the **Giardino di Poggiofanti**, a good place to unwind after a morning of following the da Sangallos.

Vignola, the Jesuits' favourite architect, was responsible for the portal on the **Palazzo Gagnoni-Grugni**, situated on Via di Voltaia, while the Medici's favoured architect, **Michelozzo**, was responsible for the façade of the church of San Agostino, located in Piazza Michelozzo. Antonio da Sangallo the Elder was the sculptor of the fine crucifix which graces the high altar.

Tempio di San Biagio **

One of the jewels of the High Renaissance, this beautifully ordered church just outside Montepulciano was begun in 1518 by **Antonio da Sangallo the Elder** and completed in 1580, after the architect's death. Its Greek cross plan is based on Bramante's design for St Peter's in Rome. There is no second tower, but with dome and cupola, its creamy walls, pediments, roofs and rounded apse, it is still elegantly poised above the rich green landscape.

From Montepulciano it's just a short drive south to the spa town of **Chianciano Terme** and the Etruscan *lucumonia*, **Chiusi**.

Above: *Small but beautiful: Tempio di San Biagio, Montepulciano.*

ANGELO AMBROGINI

One of Montepulciano's famous sons was Angelo Ambrogini (1454–94) who was born in the town and became a notable poet during the Renaissance. He changed his name to **Poliziano**, after Mons Politianus (the Roman name for Montepulciano) – the inhabitants of the settlement were known as Poliziani. From this word, Ambrogini chose his pseudonym, Poliziano. The poet was befriended by Lorenzo the Magnificent, whose life he had saved during the Pazzi assassination attempt, and enjoyed certain privileges as a result. His best-known poetic work is *Le Stanze*.

Above: *Brainchild of Pope Pius II, Pienza was purposefully laid out as a 'new town' in 1459 and is a good example of Renaissance city planning. A small hilltop town, it is one of Tuscany's most picturesque.*

SAN QUIRICO D'ORCIA

Accessible also from Montalcino (*see* page 85), this village, enclosed by 12th-century walls, is on the historic **Via Francigena**, a strategic trade route which linked Rome with prosperous northern cities in Flanders. Highlight of San Quirico is its **Collegiata**, a 12–13th-century collegiate church with a beautifully carved Romanesque portal. Frederick Barbarossa (Frederick I of Swabia) stopped here in the mid-12th century.

Pienza **

The delightfully integrated small town of Pienza was created at the request of Pope Pius II in 1459 and took just a few years to complete. The Pope, born Enea Silvio Piccolomini in Corsignano (as it was then known), transformed the town into what we see today and, during his papacy, had it renamed Pienza. Its soul is the **Piazza Pio II**, which is flanked by the Duomo, the Palazzo Piccolomini on its northern side, and the Palazzo Borghia (also known as the Palazzi Vescovile) on the southeastern side.

The architect engaged for the town's rebuilding – one of the first examples in Italy of integrated town planning – was Bernardo Rossellino (previously Leone Battista Alberti's assistant) who was also responsible for the pretty little well in the piazza. The **Duomo** boasts a fine, though austere façade which sets the tone for the interior. Aisles and a nave of equal height are relatively simple in style allowing for coloured decoration and paintings in the five chapels. Light streams in from the south and gives the cathedral an uplifting ambience.

Rossellino's best efforts were reserved, however, for the Pope's palace, the **Palazzo Piccolomini**, in which he had obviously been influenced by Alberti's designs for the Palazzo Rucellai (*see* page 51) which he completed after the elder architect's death. One side of the palace faces the piazza, the other has expansive views of the Tuscan countryside.

The **Palazzo Vescovile** now houses the **Museo Diocesano** (corso Rossellino 59, open Wednesday to Monday, mornings and afternoons in summer; mornings and afternoons, weekends only, in winter) where some excellent tapestries, paintings, sculpture, and papal and religious artifacts merit a visit.

FURTHER AFIELD

Due south of Pienza lies an area of Tuscany less frequented by tourists. For lovers of small, unspoiled Medieval villages, unusual wines and panoramic vistas, this part of Tuscany is a small gem.

Situated in the shade of Mount Amiata, **Abbadia San Salvatore** takes its name from the once-wealthy Abbey around which the town grew. The monastery dates back to the mid-8th century, but what is intact today is actually the result of construction in the 11th and 16th centuries, with some later decoration in the nave and transept.

The eastern side of *Strada Statale* No. 2 leads via many bends to **Radicofani** made famous by Boccaccio's *Decamaron*, in which he relates the incarceration of the Abbot of Cluny by local bandit, Ghino di Tacco. The village is overshadowed by the remains of its basaltic **Rocca**, of which a castellated tower stands lone sentinel to its Medieval past.

Small country roads meander southwards via Castell'Azzara to the picturesque towns of **Sorano** and nearby **Sovana**. Continuing onwards, you'll pass the tiny town of **Pitigliano**, pass a turning for **Montemerano** and arrive at the Maremma coast.

PITIGLIANO

Perched on a volcanic tufa outcrop and benefitting from an outstanding panorama, the small town of Pitigliano appears to grow out of the very rock from which it is built. Its roots stretch way back into Etruscan times, while much of the centre one sees today is Medieval. The cobble-stone streets lit by old lanterns hark back to days before electricity. Often overlooked, it was from Pitigliano that Italian landscape painter, Francesco Zuccarelli (1720–88) came. One of its unusual attractions is the **Synagogue** in the part of town known as the **Ghetto**. Jews fled 15th-century Rome and settled here, and were protected here by the Grand Dukes, out of reach of papal persecution. Persecuted again during World War II, the Jewish population today is negligible.

Left: *Light from the south window brightens the nave of Pienza's Duomo.*

Southeastern Tuscany at a Glance

BEST TIMES TO VISIT

The countryside is at its most attractive in either **spring** or early **autumn**. Tourists crowd the various sites during summer, starting from Easter until September, but many fairs and festivals make a well-planned summer visit also worthwhile. **Winter** is bleaker but the hotels and sights far less crowded – and the thermal springs a real treat. However, note that a number of hotels and restaurants close their doors in winter (at least for a couple of months) so be sure to check by telephoning or faxing before turning up.

GETTING THERE

Access to this region by **air** is the same as the access to Florence (see page 56). From Florence, there are fast **railway** links to Arezzo and Cortona (see below for more details). By **road**, Arezzo is located just off the autostrada A1, the Milan–Rome motorway. It is also accessible by the national road N69. Arezzo is 81km (50 miles) from Florence; Cortona is 29km (18 miles) from Arezzo and 70km (44 miles) from Siena. Pienza is 61km (36 miles) from Arezzo and 52km (32 miles) from Siena. Arezzo and Cortona are both situated on the main Milan–Rome **railway**. From Florence it is a 30–80 minute journey to Arezzo (depending on the

type of train you take), and a 90–120 minute trip from Rome. The fastest intercity expresses do not always stop at Cortona or Arezzo. For all information concerning trains in Italy, consult the train service's national timetable on website: www.fs-on-line.it

GETTING AROUND

Buses run between Siena and Pienza and there are services between Arezzo, Cortona and Montepulciano. However, in this slightly more rural area, a **car** is the best way to travel. The distances between the main towns are given in Getting There (this page).

WHERE TO STAY

LUXURY

Il Chiostro di Pienza, corso Rossellino 26, Pienza, tel: 0578 748400, fax: 0578 748440. Consisting of monastic cells turned into luxury rooms (complete with vaults and frescoes), it has a lovely setting. Out of season the prices are mid-range.
Locanda dell'Amorosa, at l'Amorosa, 2km (1.25 miles) south of Sinalunga, tel: 0577 679497, fax: 0577 632001. This is a tastefully restored building with hotel rooms and apartments. It is an excellent location for exploring southeastern Tuscany.
La Chiusa, via della Madonnina 88, Montefollonico, tel: 0577 669668, fax: 0577 669593.

This elegant country guesthouse has a fine restaurant and is well placed for Pienza or Montepulciano.
Brufani, piazza Italia 12, Perugia, tel: 075 5732541, fax: 075 5720210. Small hotel, some rooms with countryside views, despite being centrally located. Open year-round.

MID-RANGE

Etrusco Palace Hotel, via Fleming 39, Arezzo, tel: 0575 9984066, fax: 0575 382131. In the northwest part of town, near the centro storico, the town's most prestigious hotel, largish and modern. Ample parking.
San Michele, via Guelfa 15, Cortona, tel: 0575 604348, fax: 0575 630147. Renaissance palace turned hotel. Good location and attractive.
Castell di Ripa d'Orcia, at Castiglione d'Orcia, near San Quirico d'Orcia, tel: 0577 897376, fax: 0577 898038. A small hotel in a castle village, with good views. Simple but pleasant rooms.
Albergo Marzocco, piazza Savonarola 18, Montepulciano, tel: 0578 757262, fax: 0578 757530. Small hotel, with reasonably priced rooms.
Villa Acquaviva, strada Scansanese Nord, 1km, Montemerano, tel: 0564 602890. Delightful, small hotel (no restaurant) on a wine estate in far southeast of Tuscany.

Southeastern Tuscany at a Glance

Locanda della Posta, corso Vannucci 97, Perugia, tel: 075 5728925, fax: 075 5732562. Older hotel, medium sized, in heart of town, just off Piazza Repubblica. Good value.

Umbra, vicolo degli Archi 6, Assisi, tel: 075 812240, fax: 075 813653. Family-run hotel, smallish, right off the Piazza del Comune. Central and pleasant. Excellent value.

BUDGET

Albergo Milano, via Madonna del Prato 83, Arezzo, tel: 0575 26836. Centrally located, simple but clean hotel.

Albergo San Michele, via Guelfa 15, Cortona, tel: 0575 604348. Pleasant old mansion, good views, just two minutes from heart of *centro storico*. Has some inexpensive rooms.

La Fortezza, vicolo della Fortezza 2/b, Assisi, tel: 075 812418. Simple, small and clean. Has a well-priced restaurant which is open also to non-residents.

La Palazzina, località Le Vigne Est, Celle sul Rigo, 6km, Radicofani. *See* Where to Eat.

WHERE TO EAT

LUXURY

Il Falconiere, at San Martino a Bocena, 3km north on Castiglione Fiorentino road, near Cortona, tel: 0575 612679, fax: 0575 612927. Excellent restaurant just outside town, with pricey rooms.

La Grotta, località San Biagio 16, near Montepulciano, tel: 0578 757607. Beautiful old building and a fine reputation for its cuisine.

La Chiusa, Montefollonico, *see* Where to Stay.

Da Caino, via della Chiesa 4, Montemerano, tel: 0564 602817. Michelin-rated restaurant, reservations necessary. In far southeast of Tuscany.

MID-RANGE

La Buca di San Francesco, piazza Umberto I, Arezzo, tel: 0575 23271. Well-established restaurant, popular with locals and tourists alike.

Antica Trattoria da Guido, via Madonna del Prato 85, Arezzo, tel: 0575 23760. Cosy restaurant featuring Tuscan and Calabrian cuisine.

Enoteca Ristorante Antico Frantoio, piazza Solferino 7, Montemerano, tel: 0564 602615. In a converted wine mill, now *enoteca* for wine tasting, and good restaurant.

La Palazzina, località Le Vigne Est, Celle sul Rigo, 6km, Radicofani, tel/fax: 0578 55771. Good restaurant, serving home-grown produce; there are also a handful of budget-priced rooms available in this 17th-century hilltop hunting lodge.

BUDGET

Le Tastevin, via de' Cenci 9, Arezzo, tel: 0575 28304. Excellent restaurant offering a value-for-money set menu.

La Grotta, piazzetta Baldelli 3, Cortona, tel: 0575 630271. Excellent value and a popular restaurant with locals.

La Corte, Relais la Fattoria, via Rigone 1, Castel Rigone, tel: 075 845322, fax: 075 845197. Midway between Cortona and Perugia, manor house in centre of Medieval town. Excellent menu and also some 30 rooms.

Dal Mi' Cocco, corso Garibaldi 12, Perugia, tel: 075 5732511. Small and pleasant with a good range of inexpensive dishes. Reservations advised.

SHOPPING

This is a region of wines, olive oil, pottery and leather goods. Most tourists opt for food produce, often beautifully presented in gift packages. There is an excellent range of shops in Arezzo and Perugia, the largest towns, for seeking out fashion goods and household wares, while shoes and bags can easily be found in all the major towns.

USEFUL CONTACTS

APT, piazza della Repubblica 28, Arezzo, tel: 0575 377678.
APT, via Nazionale 42, Cortona, tel: 0575 630352.
APT, piazza del Comune 12, Assisi, tel: 075 812534.
APT, piazza 4 Novembre 3, Perugia, tel: 075 5723327.
Ufficio Informazioni, corso Rossellino 59, Pienza, tel: 0578 749071.

6
Coastal Tuscany

Fringed by the coast, Western Tuscany runs from the provincial border of La Spezia in the north along the coastal plains to the Lazio border in the south. It was one of the first inhabited areas of Tuscany. The Etruscans established settlements and created a network of city-states which, some 500 years later, were gradually overrun by the burgeoning Roman Empire. From these eras, there are numerous remains, especially in **Volterra** (*see* page 82), Pisa, Lucca and the southern parts of the Maremma.

Today's traveller heads for **Lucca**, once an Etruscan then a Roman settlement, but more important in Medieval and Renaissance times, and **Pisa**, almost exclusively known for its Leaning Tower. However, Pisa boasts a wealth of other fine monuments which should be explored.

North of Lucca, the attractions veer away from the past and concentrate on the present. The beach resorts of **Viareggio**, Pietrasanta, **Forte dei Marmi** and Marina di Massa draw the summer crowds like some kind of marine magnet and during the peak season, the beach becomes the social centre for holidaying Tuscans and tourists alike.

The coastal islands, the **Tuscan Archipelago**, are popular in summer. Protected in part by the **Parco Nazionale dell'Archipelago Toscano**, the accessible islands, such as **Elba** and **Giglio**, are visually enchanting. The land further south, once malaria-ridden, is now increasingly frequented. The **Maremma** area, unfolding between the **Metalliferous Mountains** and the sea, is Tuscany's wild west: an area of livestock, of savage beauty and one which has not been spoiled by the advances of tourism.

DON'T MISS

*** Pisa: the Leaning Tower, the Duomo, the Baptistry and the Camposanto cemetery.
*** Lucca: magnificent churches – San Michele in Foro, and San Frediano.
** Elba: a beautiful island with a place in history.
* Forte dei Marmi: visit this chic beach resort.
* Maremma: the Parco Naturale della Maremma.
* Carrara: site of the famous marble quarries, from which Michelangelo and other notable sculptors selected their white stone.

Opposite: *Popular Marciana Marina on the island of Elba.*

GRASSY RAMPARTS

Lucca is one of the few towns in Italy to have its city walls still intact. The first walls date back to Roman days while what we see today dates, in part, from the 12th century and mostly from the 17th century when the town was under threat from Florence and the Duchy of Este. The 12m-high (40ft) ramparts swell into ten arrow-shaped bastions and one smaller lookout post. Thanks to the Bourbons, the ramparts have been converted into a tree-lined promenade which overlooks the grassy spaces separating modern Lucca from the old city walls.

Opposite: *The focal point of Lucca is Piazza San Michele in Foro.*
Below: *A statue of composer Giacomo Puccini, Lucca's favourite son.*

LUCCA

A city fortified by its now-grassy Renaissance ramparts and bastions, Lucca's history goes back even further than the Renaissance to the **Etruscans**, and even into prehistory. The **Romans** bequeathed the orderly town plan when they took the city in the beginning of the second century BC and **Christianity** converted the first town in Tuscany to the faith. For over 200 years Lucca was the headquarters for the invaders (*see* page 12) rising in prosperity and power in the Middle Ages, though falling under the control of Pisa for a decade. It is from this era that much of the heart of this lovely city dates. Thanks to silk and banking, Lucca became a solid city-state during the **Renaissance** years and such was its independence, it was only incorporated into Tuscany in the 19th century.

Although several noteworthy people were born in Lucca, it is **Giacomo Puccini** (1858–1924), the composer of operas such as *Tosca* and *Madama Butterfly*, who is the most internationally renowned (*see* panel, page 108).

Lucca retains much of its **Medieval** and **Renaissance ambience** thanks to its political stability over the centuries. Its distinctive style of architecture, influenced by Pisa, is still very apparent and despite being a mid-sized city, its *centro storico* is easy to explore by foot.

San Michele in Foro ★★★

The oldest extant Romanesque church in Lucca, San Michele in Foro was built on the remains of the Roman Forum, and is in the piazza of the same name. It is the heart of the town and its social centre.

The original building was begun in the 8th century though much of what we see today is from the 11–14th centuries. Its fabulous and unusual **façade** – tiers of marvellously decorated, pencil-thin columns, multi-coloured marble capitals and rounded arches – is capped by a powerful statue of **Archangel Michael**, wings open, flanked on either side of the roof by two smaller angels. As fancy as the exterior is, the interior is contrastingly plain. Look for the **Luca della Robbia** terracotta.

Just a couple of metres along Via di Poggio, at corte San Lorenzo 8, is the **Casa Natale di Puccini**, birthplace of the Italian composer (open daily, except Monday, in summer; open mornings and afternoons the rest of the year). This is where the musician spent his early years, and memorabilia help bring the achievements and époque of this famous Lucchese to life.

Pinacoteca Nazionale ★

Art lovers should head westwards down Via di Poggio to Via Galli Tassi where the 17th-century **Palazzo Mansi** (open daily except Monday), houses a fine art gallery, tapestries and displays of period furniture. Many of its large canvases are by 15th- and 16th-century Italian masters, such as works by **Leandro Bassano** (*Landscape in Winter*), **Beccafumi** (*Portrait of Scipio*), **Bronzino** (*Cosimo I* and the young *Don Garzia de' Medici*), **Domenichino**, **Luca Giordano** (*San Sebastiano*), **Salvator Rosa** (various battle scenes) and **Veronese** (*St Peter the Hermit before the Venetian Council*).

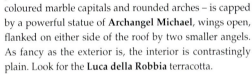

CARRARA

At the northwestern extremity of Tuscany, in the Apuan Alps, lies the sizeable town of Carrara. Some 126km (74 miles) from Florence, its three surrounding valleys have for over two millennia, been one of the world's premium centres for cutting fine-grained, white marble. Michelangelo used to work here on his sculptures, indeed, many of Florence, Pisa, Lucca and Siena's beautiful white marble statues started life here. So too the white marble cladding on Tuscan monuments. Even the fabulous white Marble Temple, in Bangkok, was created out of Carrara marble. Until a century ago, all quarrying was carried out by hand. The **Cave di Marmo di Fantiscritti** is probably the most impressive quarry to visit as it also offers an interesting museum outlining the history of marble quarrying.

Above right: *A fine mosaic
graces the eastern front of
San Frediano, Lucca.*

San Frediano ***

San Frediano is located on the northern side of the old
town, next to the **Baluarte San Frediano**, the bastion
which was named for this Romanesque church. San
Frediano is dominated by a crenellated tower but most
people are attracted by its unusual façade. Held aloft on
thin columns is a vast flat, golden mosaic depicting the
Ascension of Christ, and the apostles in the space below.
Created in the 13th century, it is best seen early in the
morning when the sun dances off the mosaicwork. Inside is an exceptionally fine font, the work of a talented
12th-century sculptor.

Returning towards the orderly plan of central Lucca,
take a stroll into in the rather unusual oval **Piazza
dell'Anfiteatro**. Sit a while and contemplate this space
which over 2000 years ago witnessed gladiatorial flights.
Although nothing remains of the arena, the ochre-
washed Medieval buildings around the central section
took the oval form, and access to the piazza is via
passages underneath houses lining its rim.

Take **Via Guinigi** (a street with some fine buildings)
south of Piazza San Pietro to arrive at the impressive
Casa di Guinigi, one-time brick home to the powerful
Guinigi family. Its peculiarity is its much-photographed
red brick tower on which trees thrive. Walk to Via San
Andrea to get better views of this anomaly.

Duomo **

In the lovely **Piazza San Martino**, surrounded by a potpourri of buildings, lies the town's **Duomo**, the cathedral dedicated to St Martin. Its Medieval Campanile towers over the terracotta roofs of the *centro storico*. What exists of this cathedral today dates from the 11th century and, to a greater extent, the remodelling work done in the following three centuries.

As with the other two main churches in Lucca, its façade is its strongest feature. Laboriously carved **Romanesque sculpture**, in a good state of conservation, decorate this asymmetrical western front. Delicate columns, trademark of fine Romanesque architecture, were created by various sculptors, thus giving them their individuality. The arches lead you into the portico; note the *Adoration of the Magi*, possibly an early example of a relief by **Nicola Pisano**.

Two important items inside the rather gloomy cathedral shouldn't be missed: the much-venerated crucifix, the **Volto Santo**, which is said to have been begun by Nicodemus; and the richly decorated, white marble tomb of **Ilaria del Carretto Guinigi**, wife of Paolo Guinigi, one of the town's wealthy 15th-century rulers. The latter is a magnificent piece of work executed in 1406 by Sienese sculptor, **Jacopo della Quercia** (ca. 1374–1438). Other noteworthy pieces in the cathedral include the two tombs in the south transept, the *tempietto* to cover the Volto Santo and the attractive inlaid floor by local sculptor, **Matteo Civitali** (1435–1511), and a later *Last Supper* by the Venetian painter, **Jacopo Tintoretto** (1518–94).

STEP BACK IN TIME

Along fashionable Via Fillungo, there is one of Lucca's institutions: the **Antico Caffè di Simo**, via Fillungo 58, Lucca, tel: 0583 496234. Behind its wooded and curved glass shop windows, an elegant array of pastries, apéritifs and delicious snacks tempt the visitor.

Below: *The elaborate Romanesque façade of Lucca's Duomo.*

BEACH RESORTS

Bordered by the Tyrrhenian Sea, Tuscany's coast has long been exploited by visitors. The most accessible parts are north of Viareggio while the resort areas to the south, around Monte Argentario, are far more recent creations answering to the needs of a more modern clientele.

Viareggio and the North *

This traditional seaside resort was developed in the early 19th century. Purpose-built streets, some gracious hotels, bathing huts and a palm-lined promenade have all the characteristics of a *stazione balneare*, seaside resort. Many an aspiring writer and artist, strolled its streets, took the air and dipped their feet in the sea (Percy Bysshe Shelley, unfortunately, drowned here in 1822).

To the north, backed by the imposing Apuan Mountains and nestling amid pleasant pine woods, there are more resorts – Lido di Camaiore, Marina di Piestrasanta and the exclusive **Forte dei Marmi**, which is still only 105km (65 miles) from Florence. It is a pretty coast, with good beaches, though most are hidden from view by the private bathing clubs that line the shore.

Below: *The Tuscan coast attracts summer visitors.*

To the south of Viareggio and situated before the popular resorts of Marina di Pisa or Tirrenia, lies the regional park, **Parco Naturale Migliarino, San Rossore, Massaciuccoli** – an area of coastal flats and an excellent spot for birding. Remote though this park may seem, Pisa is just a couple of kilometres off its eastern extreme.

Livorno and the South *

Also known as Leghorn by the British, Livorno is a major port and from here there are ferries to

Sardinia and the Tuscan Archipelago. The town was laid out by **Bernardo Buontalenti** for the **Medici** but suffered Allied bombing in World War II. Much further south, the once sleepy villages of Castiglioncello and, in the Maremma area (*see* page 118), Populonia, near Piombino and Punta Ala have burgeoned into seaside destinations while Castiglione della Pescaia, a delightful, overgrown fishing village, has managed to become a resort without too much sacrifice.

PISA

Centuries ago, Pisa was a harbour, but subsequent silting of the River Arno cut off the city's maritime links more effectively than any invader. Initially, the Etruscans founded a small port used by the Romans as a naval base. It gained its independence in the 9th century and expanded its trading links considerably in the Middle Ages when it controlled a number of Mediterranean islands including Corsica and the Balearics. At its height, Pisa rivalled both Venice and Genoa (who was to defeat Pisa's fleet at the battle of Meloria in 1284).

Ghibelline to the last, Pisa supported the Emperor and successfully stood up to its Guelf counterparts in Florence, Siena and Lucca. Weakened through internal conflict, however, the town was taken by Florence in 1406 and settled into less mercantile and bellicose activities, developing a more cultural atmosphere. Its university was inaugurated in the 14th century and one of its most famous students was astronomer, **Galileo Galilei** (1564–1642) who is reputed to have used the angle of the Leaning Tower to demonstrate the theory that, under perfect conditions, all items of a similar weight fall at a similar speed irrespective of size. During the 19th century, Pisa was particularly popular with visiting writers from Britain.

Pisa suffered some damage during World War II when the bridges spanning the Arno were bombed, and although there are still many fascinating old buildings in town, there are also some rather less attractive examples of modern architecture.

Above: *The Baptistry in Pisa's Campo dei Miracoli.*

Campo dei Miracoli ★★★

This verdant stretch of manicured lawn at the northern end of Pisa's *centro storico*, is the perfect foil for the three dazzling, marble Romanesque buildings (open daily) which sit in its midst: the **Duomo**, **Baptistry** and the city's **Campanile**, the **Torre Pendiente**, better known as the 'Leaning Tower'. It is to this piazza that most visitors hasten, but dispersed through Pisa there are a wealth of other Medieval and Renaissance sights not to be missed.

Duomo ★★

Fusing elements of Middle Eastern and Lombardic architecture in its Latin cross form, and using local, coloured marbles for decorative effect, this elaborate cathedral building – the prototype of Pisan Romanesque architecture – was begun in 1063 though remodelled after a fire in the 17th century. The nave is lined with some 68 marble columns, executed in Classical style.

One of the most impressive sights in this cathedral is the octagonal **pulpit** by **Giovanni Pisano**, probably his finest work. Its panels show high relief scenes from the New Testament. A mosaic (*Christ flanked by the Virgin and St John*) by **Cimabue** graces the apse. There are also paintings by, among others, **Andrea del Sarto** (1486–1530) and **Giovanni Antonio Sogliani** (1491–1554).

Battistero ★★★

Directly beyond the west front of the Duomo is the round Baptistry, begun in 1153 by an architect named Diotisalvi but not finished for nearly 250 years. Recalling a regal headdress in shape, it is totally unique in style. Round, with varying arcades on the exterior and bands of black and white marble on the interior, its decoration was added later by **Nicola** and **Giovanni Pisano**.

Pride of place is the magnificent and elaborate **pulpit** by Nicola Pisano. Sculpted, signed and dated 1260, this hexagonal masterpiece comprises six panels sculpted in bold relief, depicting five scenes from the New Testament. The pulpit is supported by six plain columns, terminating in a trefoil arch.

Torre Pendiente, Leaning Tower ***

However many times you have seen this cylindrical building in photographs, and despite it being smaller than one imagines, it never fails to thrill. Its anchoring section of blind arcades, surmounted by the familiar six tiers of shallow arcades, capped by its later and narrower bell tower, are all immediately recognizable. The Tower is now 5m (16ft) off-centre (it started inclining even as it was being constructed by architect **Bonanno Pisano** in 1173) and though it seems to have stopped leaning further, at present it is not considered stable. Elaborate engineering work (*see* panel, page 112), however, will soon render it much safer for visitors.

Museo dell'Opera del Duomo *

A relatively new museum just to the southeast of the Tower (open daily), this facility now houses some of the original works that were in the Duomo, Baptistry and Camposanto. These include more sculptural works by **Nicola** and **Giovanni Pisano**, some tombs, works by **Tino da Camaino**, classical pieces and ecclesiastical artifacts.

TICKET SAVINGS

Pisa's Campo dei Miracoli monuments (Cathedral, Baptistry, Leaning Tower, Museum of the Sinopie, Monumental Cemetery and Museum of the Cathedral Works) can be visited with a multiple entrance ticket. For L3000, you can visit the Cathedral. For L13,000 you can visit the Cathedral and a choice of two museums, and for L18,000 the Cathedral and all the monuments.

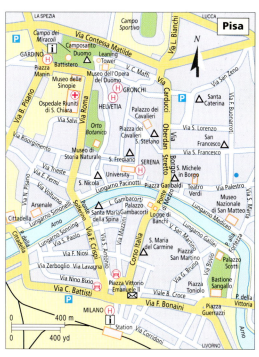

FRESCOES AND SINOPIE

Wall frescoes are created by
applying a watercolour-like
pigment onto wet, fresh
(*fresco*) plaster. However, to
do this the design must first
be drawn in outline on the
plaster (*arricciato*) foundation.
This monochrome design,
the *sinopia*, rusty in colour,
is either traced or drawn on
the wall. Then a layer of fine
plaster, *intonaco*, sufficient
for a day's work is patched
on top, the *sinopia* redrawn
and the area coloured in with
pigment. In removing frescoes
to another site, the *sinopie* are
revealed giving art historians
valuable insight into the
development of the fresco.
Pisa's **Museo delle Sinopie**
(on south side of Campo dei
Miracoli, in the 13th-century
hospice, open daily till mid-
afternoon) has been created
to exhibit the frescoes originally in the Camposanto.

Camposanto ★★

To the north of the Duomo is this famous cemetery (open daily), in use until the 18th century. Its rectangular form, behind walls of white marble, housed many important frescoes by such masters as **Benozzo Gozzoli**, **Spinello Aretino** and **Taddeo Gaddi**. One to have escaped severe damage during the bombing in World War II is the aptly named, *Triumph of Death*, a fine 14th-century work. However, most were badly damaged and today some of the remaining fragments have been detached and are displayed in the **Museo delle Sinopie**, opposite the entrance to the Duomo.

Also within the Camposanto are some fine **Roman sarcophagi**, many too damaged by the bombing, but nevertheless one of the best collections of late Roman work and one which is believed to have influenced the work of the Pisano sculptors.

Piazza dei Cavalieri ★

Vasari was responsible for redesigning the **Palazzo dei Cavalieri** in this elegant piazza, once the heart of Medieval Pisa. Named for the Knights of St Stephen (a holy military order that was created to wipe out, among other things, piracy in Pisan waters), the palace is notable for its unusual graffiti designs and also its angled façade. Today it houses part of the university and accounts for the number of young people passing time in the piazza.

Many of the streets leading from Piazza dei Cavalieri are now largely pedestrian-only. The broad pavements make walking down **Borgo Stretto** a pleasure. The shops and cafés are sheltered by 15th-century arcades though the avant-garde fashions are far from Renaissance. The street runs down to the Arno and

Below: *The Palazzo dei Cavalieri, designed by Aretine Vasari, dominates the piazza of the same name.*

across to the Risorgimento heart of today's Pisa, **Piazza Garibaldi**.

Elsewhere in Pisa there are myriad buildings and an intricate network of streets for visitors to discover. Across the bridges in the southern side of town, **Via San Martino** leads to the church of **San Martino** and takes you straight back into the Baroque era: many elegant mansions with fine façades line the street.

Keen art lovers should make time for a trip to the **Museo Nazionale di San Matteo** (Piazza San Matteo in Soarta, Lungarno Mediceo, open daily except Monday). Located in the cloisters of a former convent, it displays paintings, collections of ceramics and various pieces of sculpture. The **Palazzo Reale** (Lungarno Pacinotti 46, open mornings except Monday), located in a former Medici palace, also exhibits various collections of paintings; both are on the north banks of the *Lungarno* (which means, 'along the Arno').

Above: *The delicately Romanesque Gothic architecture of Santa Maria della Spina sits snugly, if rather incongruously, on the Arno's banks.*

Massa Marittima *

Much further south, 130km (80 miles) from Pisa and slightly inland from the coastal road, the old town of Massa Marittima still has its Medieval atmosphere and the buildings around **Piazza del Duomo** are worth the journey to this former mining town. The **Duomo** mixes elements of Pisan Romanesque and Gothic architecture; staked between the Duomo and the warmly coloured **Palazzo del Podestà**, rises the refined **Campanile**.

Situated opposite the cathedral, the *trecento* **Palazzo del Podestà** now houses an interesting archaeological museum (it is open from Tuesday to Sunday, mornings and afternoons).

ISOLA D'ELBA

Elba is the largest island in the Tuscan Archipelago, and half of it is protected by the **Parco Nazionale dell'Archipelago Toscano**. It was made famous by Napoleon's 42-week 'sojourn'. Unlike today's visitors, he left the island as soon as he possibly could. Elba was known through history for its rich iron-ore deposits, but today its natural beauty, sheltered beaches and pebbly coves, interesting flora and fauna and good tourist facilities entice visitors to its shore. Regular ferry services from Piombino make the 10km (6-mile) sea crossing in one hour.

The centre of this mountainous island rises to the granite peak, **Mount Capanne** at 1018m (3393ft). The mineral-rich mountains have provided granite, beryl, aquamarines and iron ore. The original 'Iron Port', **Portoferraio** is the main town and an industrial centre for smelting the iron ore; the second town is Marina di Campo, on the south coast. Visitors generally leave Portoferraio and make for the western part of the island where a circular route largely follows the coast below Mount Capanne.

Western Elba **

From Portoferraio a road running to the southwest climbs its way through vineyards and into the oak forested hills where you will find Napoleon's summer residence. The **Villa Napoleone di San Martino** (open during the summer season; daily

from Monday to Saturday, mornings only on Sundays and holidays) is much as it was when Napoleon left it.

Back on the main road, the town of **Marciana Marina** has developed from a small fishing port into a pleasant resort. On the flanks of Mount Capanne are the villages of **Marciana** and **Poggio**. The mountain summit is accessible by a **cable car** from which there are panoramic vistas.

Sant'Andrea, on the northern coast, is also a good place to stay for it has a pleasant, small, sandy beach and, being off the main road, is less touristy.

Marina di Campo, below the eastern flanks of the mountain, is the island's second most important centre and another pleasant resort. It is sheltered and has a very popular beach but there are also other possibilities for swimming nearby. There is a 20km (12-mile) road back to Portoferraio or a hilly road onward to Lacona and Porto Azzurro.

Eastern Elba **

There is a direct 15km (nearly 10-mile) route from Portoferraio to **Porto Azzurro**, a fine

Opposite: *Villa Napoleone di San Martino, where the Emperor Napoleon resided for just under ten months.*
Below: *Portoferraio was originally constructed for the exportation of the island's iron ore.*

Above: *Porto Azzurro attracts yachties and fishermen alike.*

port and good resort with excellent beaches nearby. A picturesque excursion from here is to **Capoliveri**, where there are panoramic views over the Golfo Stella and further to the offshore isles, Pianosa and Montecristo.

In the other direction, a road leads north through **Rio Marina** (an erstwhile mining centre and port for the shipment of ore) to **Cavo** from whence it doubles back, at a higher level, to **Rio nell'Elba** and onwards on a minor road to **Portoferraio**.

THE SOUTH

This part of Tuscany is more the domain of the beach lover, yachtie and naturalist rather than the art lover. But a combination of art and nature works very well. **Grosseto**, the provincial capital, has an old town centre which merits exploration, and then the traveller should move onwards to the Maremma, one of Tuscany's less developed areas.

The Maremma *

The Maremma is a large area, stretching all the way from the Tyrrhenian Sea to the slopes of the Monti Metalliferi, the **Metalliferous Mountains**, and the region was inhabited by the **Etruscans** (there are remains along the **River Ombrone**) and **Romans**, long before modern man managed to tame it. It is an area of flat, sometimes marshy land relieved by some hilly areas. It was prone to malaria during the Medieval era (Grand Duke Leopoldo II finally put an end to that in the early 1800s) and because of its sparse population, pirates took advantage of its isolation and thus it garnered a reputation as a dangerous and evil place. Today's residents think differently.

The *buttero*, cowboy, makes a good living and works, much as his peer in the French Camargue, herding, branding and birthing cattle. Various roads lead through the area and walkers will find a variety of interesting species, starting with a sparse maritime vegetation, passing through maquis and pine forests, and rising into deciduous forests.

The **Parco Naturale della Maremma** is a 8900ha (nearly 22,000 acres) natural park between the River Ombrone and Talamone, embracing the Monti dell'Uccellina, a range of hills. Beach-lovers head for its gorgeous sandy shores – over 20km (12 miles) long – accessible by foot from **Talamone** while nature lovers can go on organized tours in summer, or ramble at will out of season.

To the north of the Parco the forests stretch right across to **Punta Ala**, once a fine unspoiled peninsula basking in the pines, and now one boasting several luxury hotels – including an internationally acclaimed golf course – and all the trappings of a seaside resort. The beach is lovely and the marina is sheltered by the curious hook-like promontory.

In the south, near the border with Lazio, **Monte Argentario** rises from the sea to a limestone peak, aptly named **Il Telegrafo** (635m or 2090ft). It was once a separate island but is now attached to the mainland by three sandspits. Parts of it have been gazetted as a natural park for it provides a nesting ground for a number of interesting birds on the north–south migratory route.

The *strada panoramica*, scenic drive, winds its way around Argentario from **Porto Santo Stefano** (in the north) to **Porto Ercole**, in the southeast. Porto Santo Stefano is the embarkation point for visiting **Isola Giglio** and has a *seicento* Aragonese fort with good views. Porto Ercole is a small town (with Etruscan and Roman roots) which bursts into life during the summer months. Its nearby beaches and pleasure harbour make it a very popular destination.

On the middle sand spit, rising above the lagoon, lies the town of **Orbetello**; it boasts a Medieval cathedral which was constructed on the site of a former Etruscan and Roman temple.

ISOLA GIGLIO

A popular island excursion, Giglio can easily be reached from Porto Santo Stefano by a one-hour ferry ride or fast hydrofoil. It is part of the **Parco Nazionale dell'Archipelago Toscano**, and as such now protected against the burgeoning development. The island is little more than 21km² (8 sq miles) in size, its largest village being **Giglio Porto** and a secondary settlement, **Giglio Campese**, both with hotel and bed-and-breakfast accommodation. The island's sandy beaches and the vineyards attract many tourists during the Easter to mid-September season. For ferry schedules contact Toremar at Porto Santo Stefano, tel: 0564 810803.

Below: *The white, long-horned cattle of the Maremma being rounded up by a* buttero.

Coastal Tuscany at a Glance

BEST TIMES TO VISIT

The beach resorts are at their best, and busiest, in **July–Aug**. However, the climate is good also in **June** and **Sept–Oct** while **May** can be pleasant. Few hotels and restaurants are open out of the main tourist season so visitors should check ahead if they plan to visit in **winter**.

GETTING THERE

At Pisa international **airport** (Galileo Galilei, tel: 050 500707) 3km (under 2 miles) south of the town of Pisa you can catch a **train**, **bus** or hire a **car** to get to this area. The **autostrada** runs from Genoa to south of Livorno. National roads cross the provinces of Lucca, Grosseto and Livorno. Grosseto is 140km (87 miles) from Florence, 125km (78 miles) from Livorno and 85km (52 miles) from Siena. There are many smaller roads criss-crossing the three provinces but travel is relatively slow. The Genoa–Rome **railway** line passes through Viareggio, Pisa, Livorno, Piombino (on a side line) and Grosseto. From Rome to Pisa is around 3 hours, depending on the type of train.

GETTING AROUND

Car hire is easiest. **Buses** between the main cities (Lucca, Viareggio, Grosseto) are good, but infrequent to the smaller destinations. There are bus services around Elba and connecting the two main

settlements on Giglio. From Florence it is 77km (49 miles) to Pisa and 74km (36 miles) to Lucca. Pisa to Lucca is 22km (14 miles). Piombino (for Elba) is 77km (49 miles) from Grosseto, 82km (51 miles) from Livorno, and 160km (100 miles) from Florence. There are frequent sea crossings (including car **ferries**) between Piombino and Elba from Easter to mid-September, and similar **hydrofoil** and car ferry services between Porto Santo Stefano and Giglio Porto, on the isle of Giglio. The **railway** line is not very useful for a touring visitor in the southern half of these three provinces. Viareggio, Lucca and Pisa are on the Genoa–Rome line. A car is recommended.

WHERE TO STAY

LUXURY

Locanda L'Elisa, via Nuova per Pisa 1952, SS12, Massa Pisana, Lucca, tel: 0583 379737, fax: 0583 379019. Just 4.5km (3 miles) from town, small and exclusive, a few rooms and apartments, with gardens and pool. Fine restaurant.
Green Park Resort, via delle Magnolie 4, Tirrenia, tel: 050 313571, fax: 050 3135778. New, luxurious hotel with full facilities, in parkland near sea.
Grand Hotel Duomo, via Santa Maria 94, Pisa, tel: 050 561894, fax: 050 560418. A few metres from Campo dei Miracoli, or *centro storico*, city hotel with garage parking.

Hotel Byron, viale Morin 46, Forte dei Marmi, tel: 0584 787052, fax: 0584 787152. Beautiful setting for this small-ish hotel. Fine restaurant.
Plaza e de Russie, piazza d'Azeglio 1, Viareggio, tel: 0584 44449, fax: 0584 44031. Renovated period hotel with excellent rooftop restaurant.
Villa Ottone, località Ottone, Portoferraio, Elba, tel: 0565 933042, fax: 0565 933257. Open summer only, stately mid-sized hotel. Lovely setting, good restaurant.

MID-RANGE

Villa San Michele, San Michele in Escheto, off S12, 4km from Lucca, tel: 0583 370276, fax: 0583 370277. Delightful villa in peaceful village, with both rooms and apartments.
Hotel La Luna, corte Compagni 12, (off Via Fillungo), Lucca, tel: 0583 493634, fax: 0583 490021. Near amphitheatre, a fine small hotel.
Hotel Ristorante Francesco, via Santa Maria 129, Pisa, tel: 050 554109, fax: 050 556145. Small, family-run, central. Popular restaurant.
Puntoverde, viale degli Etruschi 23, Marina di Campo, Elba, tel: 0565 977482, fax: 0565 977486. Mid-sized hotel open April to mid-October. Fairly basic, but near beaches.
Baia d'Argento, località Pozzarello, 2km (1 mile) Porto Santo Stefano, tel: 0564 812643, fax: 0564 813957. Open summer only.

Coastal Tuscany at a Glance

Hotel Cernia, Sant'Andrea, Elba, tel: 0565 908194, fax: 0565 908253. Open mid-April to mid-October. Beautiful gardens, comfortable hotel.

BUDGET
Albergo Diana, via del Molinetto 11, Lucca, tel: 0583 492202, fax: 0583 467795. Small pension near San Martino. Clean and pleasant.
Hotel Amalfitana, via Roma 44, Pisa, tel: 050 29000, fax: 050 25218. 17th-century convent now small hotel with fine interior decor. Excellent value.
Hotel Lupori, via Galcani 9, Viareggio, tel: 0584 962266, fax: 0584 962267. A few blocks from beach, still in the heart of town, a small hotel with parking. Good value.
Hotel Bellavista, Sant'Andrea, Elba, tel: 0565 908015, fax: 0565 908079. Simple and basic hotel at beach resort.

WHERE TO EAT
LUXURY
Gazebo, Locanda L'Elisa, Massa Pisana, Lucca, see Where to Stay.
Puccini, corte San Lorenzo 1, Lucca, tel: 0583 316116. Excellent à la carte menu, also set menus. Good wine list.
Al Ristoro dei Vecchi Macelli, via Volturno 49, Pisa, tel: 050 20424. Towards Citadella, a popular, excellent restaurant.
La Magnolia, Hotel Byron, see Where to Stay.
La Terrazza, Plaza e de Russie, see Where to Stay.

Capo Nord, port area, località La Fenicia, Marciana Marina, Elba, tel: 0565 996983. One of the island's premiere restaurants. Reservations necessary.

MID-RANGE
Bucca di Sant'Antonio, via delle Cervia 1/5, Lucca, tel: 0583 55881. Popular, great atmosphere, menus in mid-range and budget category. Reservations recommended.
Antico Trattoria da Bruno, via Luigi Bianchi 12 (Porta Lucca), Pisa, tel: 050 560818. Popular, full of atmosphere, reservations necessary.
Il Lucumone, al Castello di Populonia, 13.5km (8 miles), Piombino, tel: 0565 29471. Overlooking bay at Populonia, north of Piombino.
Bologna, via Firenze 27, Marina di Campo, Elba, tel: 0565 9761105. Popular, fish specialities. Open summer only.

BUDGET
Trattoria da Giulio, via delle Conce 45, Lucca, tel: 0583 55948. Tuscan food. Popular, reservations recommended.
Antico Caffè di Simo, via Fillungo 58, Lucca, tel: 0583 496234. A popular old-world coffee shop and bar.
Federico Salza, borgo Stretto 46, Pisa, tel: 050 580144. A caffè renowned for its pasticceria, snacks and salads.
Al Castelleto, piazza San Felice 12, Pisa, (no phone). Bustling, popular, good value, à la carte and pizzas.

Pancino, via Duca d'Aosta 4, Forte dei Marmi, tel: 0584 81162. Central, good atmosphere and excellent-value fish.

SHOPPING
Lucca is renowned for olive oil. Wine, leather and fashion items are available in the resorts, and in the towns of Lucca and Pisa.

TOURS AND EXCURSIONS
Trips go to Elba from Piombino (contact Toremar, tel: 0565 31100) and to Giglio from Porto Santo Stefano (contact Toremar, tel: 0564 810803).

USEFUL CONTACTS
Toremar, Piazzale Premuda, Piombino, tel: 0565 31100, or Calata Italia 22, Portoferraio, tel: 0565 918080. Booking and tickets for Elba ferry.
Mobylines, Piazzale Premuda, Piombino 13, tel: 0565 221212, or Viale Elba, Portoferraio, tel: 0565 914133. Booking and tickets for Elba ferry.
Toremar, Porto Santo Stefano, piazza Candi 1, tel: 0564 810803. Booking and tickets for Giglio ferry.
APT, via Carlo Cammeo 2, Pisa, tel: 050 560464.
APT, Vecchia Porta San Donato, Piazzale Verdi, Lucca, tel: 0583 419689.
APT, viale Carducci 10, Viareggio, tel: 0584 962233.
APT, calata Italia 26, Portoferraio, tel: 0565 9144671.
APT, corso Umberto 55a, Porto Santo Stefano, tel: 0564 814208.

Travel Tips

Tourist Information

The **Ente Nazionale Italiano per il Turismo (ENIT)** is the publicity arm for promotion of Italy overseas. They are found in the UK at 1 Princes Street, London WIR 8AY, tel: 020 7408 1254, fax: 020 7493 6695; in the USA at 500 N Michigan Ave, Suite 2240, Chicago 1, Illinois 60611, tel: 312 644 0996, fax: 312 644 3019; or 630 Fifth Ave, Suite 1565, New York, NY 10111, tel: 212 245 4822, fax: 212 586 9249, and 124000 Wilshire Blvd, Suite 550, Los Angeles, CA 90025, tel: 310 820 1959, fax: 310 820 6357. In Tuscany, the **Azienda di Promozione Turistica** (APT) or tourist office is the place to find local tourist information.

Entry Requirements

Visitors with EU nationality require a valid national identity card or a passport, valid for a further 6 months after arrival. All other visitors need a valid passport. Non-EU citizens who wish to stay longer than 90 days require a visa, as do some other nationals. If in doubt, check with your local embassy.

If using your own car, bring your international driving licence (EU nationals can drive on domestic licences), the car's documents and the all-important Green Card which gives you insurance cover. This is available from your insurance company, the AA or RAC in the UK. Also, you require a red triangle which you need to position 50m (55yd) down the road, if involved in an accident or breakdown.

Customs

Custom regulations for EU citizens are fairly generous. 800 cigarettes, 200 cigars or 1kg (2.2 lb) tobacco; 10 litres (16 pints) spirits, 90 litres (about 120 standard bottles) wine and 100 litres (160 pints) of beer. For non-EU nationals, the limits are the usual: 400 cigarettes, 100 cigars, 1 litre spirits or 2 litres (just under 3 standard bottles) wine.

Health Requirements

There are no special requirements for entry into Italy. If you develop medical problems, consult the contacts given under Emergencies (see page 126).

Getting There

By air: Tuscany has two international airports: **Florence** (Amerigo Vespucci, tel: 055 30615), with frequent taxi services from airport to centre. Airlines serving this airport include Meridiana. **Pisa** has a much bigger international airport (Galileo Galilei, tel: 050 849111). Hourly trains go from Pisa airport to Florence, via the centre of Pisa. Airlines serving this airport include Alitalia, British Airways, Ryanair. **Bologna** has an international airport (Bologna-G. Marconi), and has buses to the railway station where regular train services connect it with Prato, Florence and Arezzo. Airlines serving this airport include Alitalia, British Airways, Ryanair. **Alitalia:** UK tel: 020 7602 7111; Florence tel: 055 27888; Pisa tel: 050 501570. **Meridiana:** tel: 020 7839 2222 in the UK; tel: 055 32961 in Florence. **British Airways:** tel: 0845 7733377 in the UK; tel: 050 501838 in Pisa, tel: 848812266 (toll reduced) throughout Italy. **Ryanair:** tel: 054 156 9569 in UK, website: www.ryanair.com

Visitors from the USA need to fly to Milan or Rome with international airlines, and transfer to the local airlines, Alitalia or Meridiana, to arrive in Tuscany.

By rail: The **Ferrovie dello Stato**, Italian State Railway network, spans over 16,000km (10,000 miles), linking the borders with France, Switzerland and Austria and onward via ferries to Sardinia and Sicily in the south. Foreigners can buy special tickets such as Eurodomino (permitting 3, 5 or 10 full calendar days' travel, unlimited mileage within each specified day, for a month after first date used) at stations on proof of foreign residency. Two main lines serve Tuscany: Turin–Genoa–Viareggio–Grosseto–Rome and Milan–Bologna–Florence–Arezzo–Rome. From Bologna it takes 57 minutes by fast train; from Milan, just over 3 hours, and from Rome 94 minutes. All tickets must be validated by a punchmark from a machine found on or near the platform. Information can be obtained in the UK from Citalia, tel: 020 8686 0677, fax: 8681 0712.

By road: Italy has a good network of roads and motorways (*autostrade*) indicated by green signs. Florence is on the toll-paying *Autostrada del Sole*, the A1, which links Milan via Bologna and skirting Florence to Rome and Naples. For speed, take the toll-paying *autostrade*, but for pleasure, stick to the *strade statali* (state roads) and the smaller bi-roads. *Globetrotter Travel Map of Florence and Tuscany* shows alternative routes.

ROAD SIGNS

senso unico • one-way street
Alto • Stop
Avanti • Go (on pedestrian crossing)
Sottopassaggio • pedestrian underpass
Passo carribile • Don't park here – the entrance is constantly in use
Benzina • petrol/gas
Fermata • bus stop
Uscita • exit
Questura • police station
autostrada • motorway
pedaggio • toll
Accendere i fari • turn your lights on
Curva molto pericolosa • very dangerous bend

Visitors arriving by private car must carry the vehicle's documents and their driving licence, and require valid insurance cover – the Green Card.

What to Pack

In winter (Nov–March), bring warm clothing, umbrella and a light rain jacket. Budget and moderate hotels aren't always well heated so bring warm bedwear and extra socks. Spring and autumn days can be cool or warm, so layered clothing is best. A showerproof jacket is useful. Summer clothing should be light with a jacket for evenings. Most restaurants, except the most exclusive, don't require tie and jacket, but since Florentines love dressing up you'll feel more comfortable if you do too. For lovers of art history, trainers or flat shoes are most suitable for walking.

Bring binoculars to see the often high up and poorly lit works. Pack a separate purse containing the change needed to light chapels and churches.

Money Matters

Until the Euro is fully operative, the Italian currency is still the *lira*, plural, *lire*, sometimes written with the sign £ or L. A single *lira* is worth practically nothing. The currency starts to have value when you speak of 1000s. Small coins are useful for tips, church lighting and some phone cabins. Exchange rates with most EU currencies are now fixed – the UK Pound is still one of the exceptions – and so rates for this and those other non-fixed currencies fluctuate daily. To exchange money, use one of the exchange offices where you see the sign *cambio*, as the service is far simpler than that of a bank. The easiest way of obtaining currency is an ATM (Automatic Teller Machine), called a *Bancomat* in Italy, with your credit card (Mastercard, Visa, etc.) and pin number.

Accommodation

There is accommodation to suit most purses. Be prepared for higher prices than in other European provincial towns. The top-of-the-range *alberghi* hotels in Florence can be as expensive as those in Milan or Rome. However, there is plenty of mid-range and some budget accommodation. *Agriturismo* – rural accommodation – is a growing sector. For full details, visit the website www.agriturismo.regione.toscana.it

Pensioni can be a good option; some are quite luxurious. At the bottom of the budget are *Residenze*, even more basic. The costs for a double room are calculated as follows: Budget: Less than 80 Euros or L160,000 (at the lower prices, bathrooms are often shared); Mid-range: 90–145 Euros or L180,000–290,000 (these include private facilities) Luxury: 150–225 Euros or L300,000–450,000.

All the cities of Tuscany fill up with holidaymakers in summer (June–Sept) while Tuscan families take to the beaches. At this time is it essential to have secured a reservation for accommodation. Easter is likewise busy. Some hotels close from October to Easter.

Eating Out

In a region renowned for its cuisine, eating out is a pastime to which Tuscans will devote their unstinting attention and their wallets. There are some remarkably good, traditional restaurants both in and outside the towns, but few are inexpensive. *Ristoranti* (with both a good menu and an expansive wine list, are the most expensive; *trattorie* prices depend on location and clientele. Other alternatives include the *enoteche* (*enoteca* means 'wine bar') which over the last decade have become fashionable places to eat, too. For less expensive options look at a *tavola calda* or a *pizzeria*, some of which sell take-away pizza slices. Note that many restaurants close in August, and at least 1–2 days a week.

For a fine meal without wine at a luxury restaurant, expect to pay over 50 Euros or L100,000; for a mid-range restaurant, 30–45 Euros or L60,000–90,000; and for a budget meal, less than 25 Euros or L50,000.

Transport

Italy has good public transport systems and the region of Tuscany is no exception.
Air: There is no air transport within Tuscany; there is air transport from Rome or Milan to Florence and Pisa. For more details, *see* Getting There.
Rail: Pisa, Prato, Siena and Arezzo are all accessible by train from Florence. Running along the coast, from Genoa to Rome, the railway links Viareggio in the north with Grosseto in the south. The *Ferrovie dello Stato*, State Railways, offers various reduced price tickets (the Italy Railcard, for example, permits 8, 15, 21 or 30 days' unlimited travel in 1st or 2nd class, from around US$210 upwards). Details on the railway services can be found (in English also) at www.fs-on-line.com

Bus: The intercity bus services are good, especially between the larger towns. Information can be obtained from **CAP**, largo Fratelli Alinari 9, Florence, tel: 055 214637; **Lazzi**, via Paisiello 13r, Florence, tel: 055 355305, website: www.lazzi.it **SITA**, via Santa Caterina da Siena 15, Florence, tel: 055 214721; or from the Tourist Office in your home country.
Car: Car rental is available at the airports and in Florence town centre. The A1 *autostrada* serves Florence and Arezzo. The A11 runs from Florence via Lucca to Viareggio where it links with the A12, northbound to Genoa and southbound via Pisa to Rosignano. There are also *superstrade*, fast highways that link towns: Florence to Siena, for instance.
All drivers must carry driver's licences, wear seat belts, drive in shoes and have a red warning triangle in case of accident or breakdown. Speed limits are 110kph (68mph) on major roads and 130kph (81mph) on the *autostrade*. Spot fines may be administered by the police to speeding drivers.

CONVERSION CHART		
From	**To**	**Multiply By**
Millimetres	Inches	0.0394
Metres	Yards	1.0936
Metres	Feet	3.281
Kilometres	Miles	0.6214
Square kilometres	Square miles	0.386
Hectares	Acres	2.471
Litres	Pints	1.760
Kilograms	Pounds	2.205
Tonnes	Tons	0.984
To convert Celsius to Fahrenheit: x 9 ÷ 5 + 32		

If driving a private car, an anti-theft steering wheel lock is a relatively inexpensive deterrent against car theft.

Business Hours

Food shops and markets open around 07:30, closing for lunch around 12:30–13:00. Shops re-open in the afternoon around 16:00 until 19:00 or later. Fashion stores, open Mon–Sat, rarely open before 10:30. Some close for lunch. Others remain open till 19:00–20:00. Banks open Mon–Fri 08:30–13:30 and again 14:30–15:30. They close at weekends. ATM outlets are open 24 hours a day. Museums and monuments are generally open 9:00–19:00 Tues–Sat, with a two-hour lunch break, and 9:00–13:00 on Sunday. Some private galleries close weekly on a day other than Monday. Most have different winter and summer timetables. Few open on public holidays. Churches generally open early in the morning, around 7:00, closing at 18:00. Many churches close between 12:00 and 16:00.

Time Difference

Italy is GMT +1 in winter, and GMT +2 in summer. So at 12 noon in London in December, it is 13:00 in Tuscany. The 24-hour clock is used.

Communications

Mail from Italy can be slow except for the new 24-hour delivery service (at a price). Stamps can be bought from tabacchi (tobacconists) who are open longer hours than La Posta (the post office). For

packages and other mail, the *Ufficio Postale Centrale* (Main Post Office) in Florence, via Pellicceria 3, is open Mon–Fri 08:30–13:20, Sat 08:30–12:00. Every second Italian seems to have a mobile **telephone**, but there are still plenty of public phones operated by coins or prepaid *schede* or *carte telephoniche* (telephone cards) available from newsstands, post offices or *tabacchi*. Some telephone cabins accept inter-

GOOD READING

• Boccaccio, Giovanni (1995) *Decameron*, translated by GH McWilliam. Penguin.
• Forster, EM (2000) *A Room with a View*. Penguin.
• Hibbert, Christopher (1979) *The Rise and Fall of the House of Medici*. Penguin.
• Machiavelli, Niccolò (1988) *The Prince*, translated by Bruce Penman. Cambridge University Press.
• Mayes, Francis (1996) *Under the Tuscan Sun*. Bantam Books.
• Origo, Iris (1992) *The Merchant of Prato*. Peregrine Books.
• Murray, Linda and Peter (1963) *The Art of the Renaissance*. Thames and Hudson.
• Parker, Allan (2000) *Seasons in Tuscany*. Penguin.
• Stone, Irving (1989) *The Agony and the Ecstasy*. Mandarin.
• Vasari, Giorgio (1965) *Lives of the Artists*, translated by George Bull. Penguin.

national credit cards and others can even send faxes. Italy has Home Direct Dialling and toll-free numbers will link you with AT&T, Telstra, MCI, British Telecom and other international systems for debiting calls to your home account. All numbers in Italy start with 0 unless they are freephone numbers. Unlike the practices in some countries, you must always dial the 0 and the code, whether you are in the same town or overseas. Dialling codes are as follows: Florence 055, Pisa 050, Siena 0577, and Lucca 0583, all followed by the subscriber's number. To call overseas, dial 00 followed by the country code and then the city or area code without the 0 before it, and the subscriber's number (for instance, to London could be 00 44 20 7 or 8 plus the subscriber's number). Dialling to Italy from overseas, you need to keep the 0 of the dial code in the number. **Faxes** can be sent from the post office, and also from a lot of phone cabins around town. Italy is increasingly tuned into the **Internet**. In Florence, Siena, Pisa and Lucca there are plenty of inexpensive cyber-cafés for e-mail and surfing.

Electricity

The current in Italy is 220V AC and two-pin, round plugs are used. Buy adapters at electrical stores or at large airports.

Weights and Measures

Italy follows the metric system. When buying food in delis, cold meats are often sold by the *etto*, 100g (3.4oz) units.

Health Precautions

Tap water in Florence is safe, if not particularly pleasant, but bottled mineral water is available. In summer, bring sunscreen and mosquito repellent. Medical facilities are good but expensive. Take out medical insurance for your trip. If you come from an EU country, you may be eligible for free emergency medical care under EU regulations, but you require Form E111 to benefit from this. Obtain and validate one from your local post office before leaving home. For first aid, *pronto soccorso*, go to the outpatients department of the local hospital, or the railway station and airport. Dial **113** for an emergency.

Personal Safety

Petty theft is Italy's main drawback. Bag snatching and pickpocketing are rife in tourist areas and on crowded buses and trains during peak times. Carry cash and credit cards in a money belt. Be aware at all times. Carry a photocopy of your passport in your wallet and leave the passport, air tickets and other valuables in safe keeping at your hotel. If driving around Tuscany, you will sometimes have to leave your car quite far from hotels or sights so do not leave anything visible inside the car.

Emergencies

Report robberies immediately to the *Carabinieri* (military police) at their *caserma*, or to the *polizia* (civil police) at the *questura*, or telephone the emergency number, tel: **113**.

For fire emergencies, tel: **115** and for breakdown assistance on the road, tel: **116**. For medical assistance in English, tel: 06 8080995, and for health emergencies, tel: **118**.

Etiquette

Politeness is still appreciated and a *Buon giorno, grazie* and *arrivederci* at the appropriate moment are always welcome. As is handshaking, and a polite *piacere* on being introduced to someone. Decorum is expected in religious buildings. Swimwear is taboo and skimpy shorts and T-shirts are frowned on, though Bermuda shorts and bare shoulders seem to be accepted nowadays. Topless sunbathing is outlawed but the ruling not enforced.

Tipping

Some expensive restaurants take the decision out of your hands and add an automatic 10–15 per cent on to bills. The rest rely on the client's benevolence. There is no obligation to tip, and you can even ask for the automatic 10 per cent to be removed and tip at your own discretion. Most Italians will leave a small gratuity in a simple restaurant (rounding up the bill to a convenient sum), while tourists either leave none or too much.

Language

Apart from the national language, Italian, most Italians involved in the tourist industry also speak English and French. Florentine Italian is considered the best in Italy, hence the proliferation of language schools.

INDEX